Give'em & Bake'em - Recipes in a Mug!

Mug 'Ems make great gifts for your family and friends. Use the recipes in this book to assemble your homemade gift. Place the ingredients in a ziplock or food-safe bag and set the sealed bag in a decorative mug. Each recipe includes gift tags for your convenience – just cut them out, fold and personalize. Attach the personalized tag to the mug and decorate with ribbon, fabric and raffia.

When making these homemade gifts, use mugs that hold a volume of at least 1½ cups. For safety reasons, it is important that you do not give your gift in a metal or plastic mug.

Printed in the United States of America
by G&R Publishing Co.

Distributed By:

507 Industrial Street
Waverly, IA 50677

ISBN-13: 978-1-56383-202-4
ISBN-10: 1-56383-202-X
Item #3774

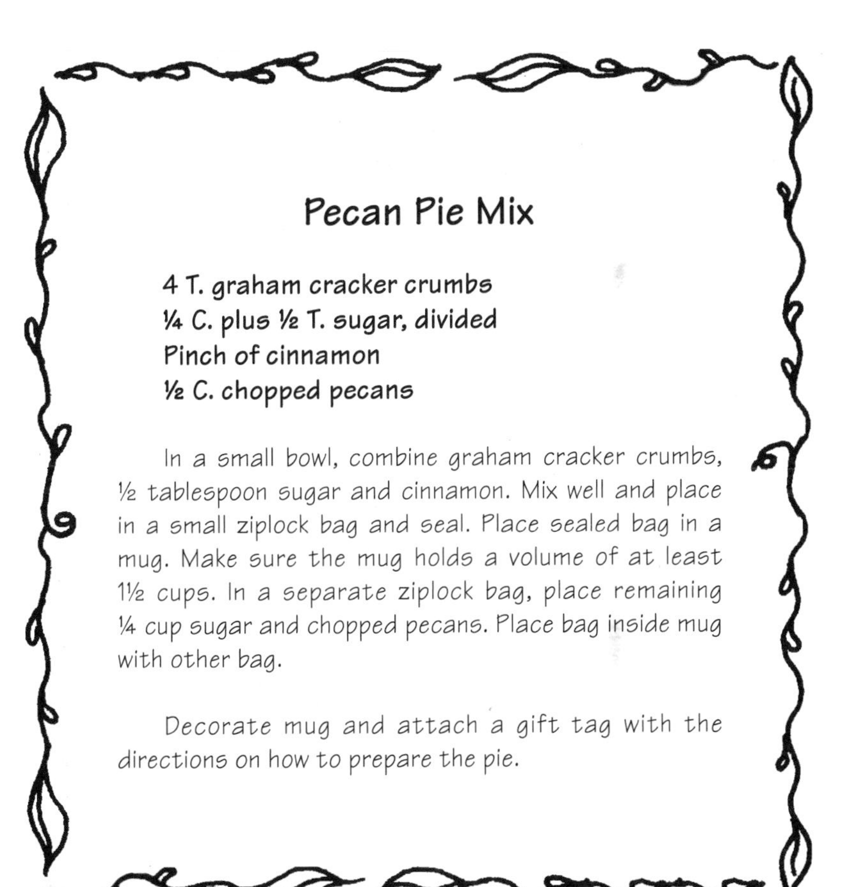

Pecan Pie Mix

4 T. graham cracker crumbs
¼ C. plus ½ T. sugar, divided
Pinch of cinnamon
½ C. chopped pecans

In a small bowl, combine graham cracker crumbs, ½ tablespoon sugar and cinnamon. Mix well and place in a small ziplock bag and seal. Place sealed bag in a mug. Make sure the mug holds a volume of at least 1½ cups. In a separate ziplock bag, place remaining ¼ cup sugar and chopped pecans. Place bag inside mug with other bag.

Decorate mug and attach a gift tag with the directions on how to prepare the pie.

Gift tag directions:
Pecan Pie

4 T. butter, melted, divided
Pecan Pie Mix
1 egg
½ tsp. vanilla
¼ C. light corn syrup

Preheat oven to 350°. To make crust, in a small bowl, combine 2 tablespoons melted butter with contents of bag containing graham cracker crumbs. Mix well and press mixture into bottom and halfway up sides of lightly greased mug. Bake in oven for 5 to 8 minutes. Meanwhile, in a separate bowl, combine contents of remaining bag with remaining 2 tablespoons melted butter, egg, vanilla and light corn syrup. Mix for 1 minute, until smooth. Allow crust to cool slightly and pour pecan mixture over crust in mug. Bake for 15 to 20 minutes. Enjoy!

Pecan Pie

4 T. butter, melted, divided
Pecan Pie Mix
1 egg
½ tsp. vanilla
¼ C. light corn syrup

Preheat oven to 350°. To make crust, in a small bowl, combine 2 tablespoons melted butter with contents of bag containing graham cracker crumbs. Mix well and press mixture into bottom and halfway up sides of lightly greased mug. Bake in oven for 5 to 8 minutes. Meanwhile, in a separate bowl, combine contents of remaining bag with remaining 2 tablespoons melted butter, egg, vanilla and light corn syrup. Mix for 1 minute, until smooth. Allow crust to cool slightly and pour pecan mixture over crust in mug. Bake for 15 to 20 minutes. Enjoy!

Pecan Pie

4 T. butter, melted, divided
Pecan Pie Mix
1 egg
½ tsp. vanilla
¼ C. light corn syrup

Preheat oven to 350°. To make crust, in a small bowl, combine 2 tablespoons melted butter with contents of bag containing graham cracker crumbs. Mix well and press mixture into bottom and halfway up sides of lightly greased mug. Bake in oven for 5 to 8 minutes. Meanwhile, in a separate bowl, combine contents of remaining bag with remaining 2 tablespoons melted butter, egg, vanilla and light corn syrup. Mix for 1 minute, until smooth. Allow crust to cool slightly and pour pecan mixture over crust in mug. Bake for 15 to 20 minutes. Enjoy!

fold
You've
Been
Mugged!
MUG'EMS
by
CQ Products
www.cqproducts.com
You've
Been
Mugged!
MUG'EMS
by
CQ Products
www.cqproducts.com

Pecan Pie

4 T. butter, melted, divided
Pecan Pie Mix
1 egg
½ tsp. vanilla
¼ C. light corn syrup

Preheat oven to 350°. To make crust, in a small bowl, combine 2 tablespoons melted butter with contents of bag containing graham cracker crumbs. Mix well and press mixture into bottom and halfway up sides of lightly greased mug. Bake in oven for 5 to 8 minutes. Meanwhile, in a separate bowl, combine contents of remaining bag with remaining 2 tablespoons melted butter, egg, vanilla and light corn syrup. Mix for 1 minute, until smooth. Allow crust to cool slightly and pour pecan mixture over crust in mug. Bake for 15 to 20 minutes. Enjoy!

Pecan Pie

4 T. butter, melted, divided
Pecan Pie Mix
1 egg
½ tsp. vanilla
¼ C. light corn syrup

Preheat oven to 350°. To make crust, in a small bowl, combine 2 tablespoons melted butter with contents of bag containing graham cracker crumbs. Mix well and press mixture into bottom and halfway up sides of lightly greased mug. Bake in oven for 5 to 8 minutes. Meanwhile, in a separate bowl, combine contents of remaining bag with remaining 2 tablespoons melted butter, egg, vanilla and light corn syrup. Mix for 1 minute, until smooth. Allow crust to cool slightly and pour pecan mixture over crust in mug. Bake for 15 to 20 minutes. Enjoy!

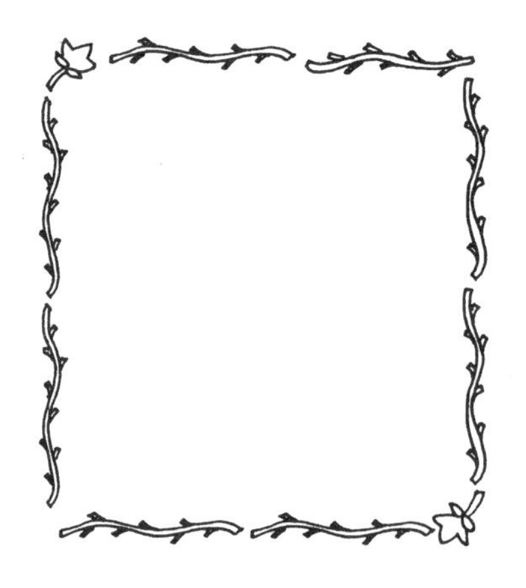

← fold →

You've
Been
Mugged!

MUG'EMS
by
CQ Products
www.cqproducts.com

You've
Been
Mugged!

MUG'EMS
by
CQ Products
www.cqproducts.com

Tapioca Pudding Mix

1½ T. quick cooking tapioca
1 T. raisins
1 T. golden raisins
2 T. sugar

In a small bowl, combine above ingredients. Mix well and place in a sandwich-size ziplock bag and seal. Place sealed bag in a mug. Make sure the mug holds a volume of at least 1½ cups.

Decorate mug and attach a gift tag with the directions on how to prepare the pudding.

Gift tag directions:
Tapioca Pudding

1⅛ C. milk
Tapioca Pudding Mix
1 egg yolk
½ tsp. vanilla

Place milk in mug. Heat milk in microwave until simmering, about 1½ to 2 minutes. Add Tapioca Pudding Mix from bag, mix well and return to microwave for an additional 2 to 3 minutes, being careful not to let mixture boil. In a small bowl, combine egg yolk and vanilla. Add 2 tablespoons of the heated tapioca mixture to the egg yolk mixture. Stir well and return egg yolk mixture to mug with remaining tapioca mixture. Return to microwave for an additional minute. Cover and chill in refrigerator. Enjoy!

Tapioca Pudding

1⅛ C. milk
Tapioca Pudding Mix
1 egg yolk
½ tsp. vanilla

Place milk in mug. Heat milk in microwave until simmering, about 1½ to 2 minutes. Add Tapioca Pudding Mix from bag, mix well and return to microwave for an additional 2 to 3 minutes, being careful not to let mixture boil. In a small bowl, combine egg yolk and vanilla. Add 2 tablespoons of the heated tapioca mixture to the egg yolk mixture. Stir well and return egg yolk mixture to mug with remaining tapioca mixture. Return to microwave for an additional minute. Cover and chill in refrigerator. Enjoy!

Tapioca Pudding

1⅛ C. milk
Tapioca Pudding Mix
1 egg yolk
½ tsp. vanilla

Place milk in mug. Heat milk in microwave until simmering, about 1½ to 2 minutes. Add Tapioca Pudding Mix from bag, mix well and return to microwave for an additional 2 to 3 minutes, being careful not to let mixture boil. In a small bowl, combine egg yolk and vanilla. Add 2 tablespoons of the heated tapioca mixture to the egg yolk mixture. Stir well and return egg yolk mixture to mug with remaining tapioca mixture. Return to microwave for an additional minute. Cover and chill in refrigerator. Enjoy!

fold

You've
Been
Mugged!

MUG'EMS
by
CQ Products
www.cqproducts.com

You've
Been
Mugged!

MUG'EMS
by
CQ Products
www.cqproducts.com

Tapioca Pudding

1⅛ C. milk
Tapioca Pudding Mix
1 egg yolk
½ tsp. vanilla

Place milk in mug. Heat milk in microwave until simmering, about 1½ to 2 minutes. Add Tapioca Pudding Mix from bag, mix well and return to microwave for an additional 2 to 3 minutes, being careful not to let mixture boil. In a small bowl, combine egg yolk and vanilla. Add 2 tablespoons of the heated tapioca mixture to the egg yolk mixture. Stir well and return egg yolk mixture to mug with remaining tapioca mixture. Return to microwave for an additional minute. Cover and chill in refrigerator. Enjoy!

Tapioca Pudding

1⅛ C. milk
Tapioca Pudding Mix
1 egg yolk
½ tsp. vanilla

Place milk in mug. Heat milk in microwave until simmering, about 1½ to 2 minutes. Add Tapioca Pudding Mix from bag, mix well and return to microwave for an additional 2 to 3 minutes, being careful not to let mixture boil. In a small bowl, combine egg yolk and vanilla. Add 2 tablespoons of the heated tapioca mixture to the egg yolk mixture. Stir well and return egg yolk mixture to mug with remaining tapioca mixture. Return to microwave for an additional minute. Cover and chill in refrigerator. Enjoy!

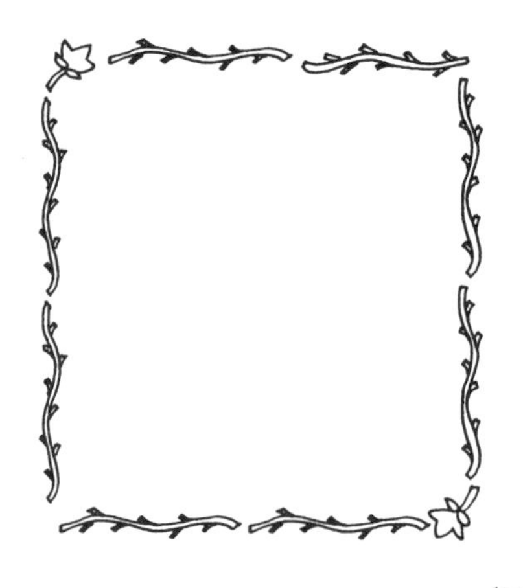

← fold →

You've
Been
Mugged!

MUG'EMS
by
CQ Products
www.cqproducts.com

You've
Been
Mugged!

MUG'EMS
by
CQ Products
www.cqproducts.com

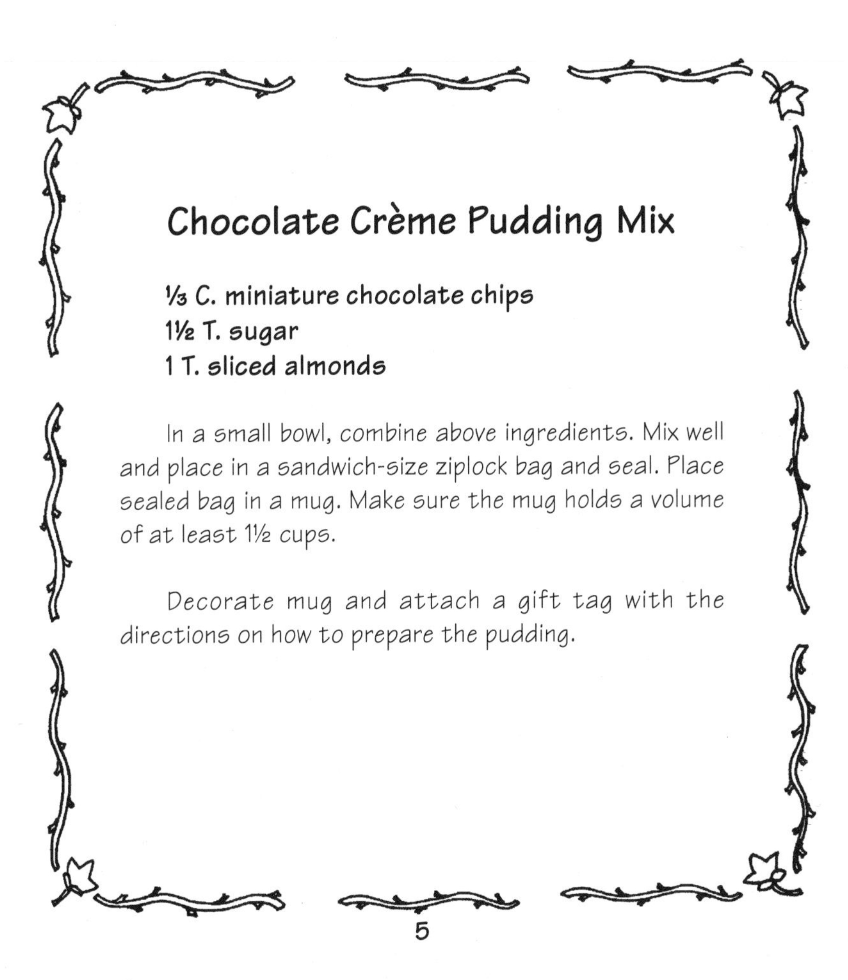

Chocolate Crème Pudding Mix

⅓ C. miniature chocolate chips
1½ T. sugar
1 T. sliced almonds

In a small bowl, combine above ingredients. Mix well and place in a sandwich-size ziplock bag and seal. Place sealed bag in a mug. Make sure the mug holds a volume of at least 1½ cups.

Decorate mug and attach a gift tag with the directions on how to prepare the pudding.

Gift tag directions:
Chocolate Crème Pudding

¾ C. whole milk or half n' half
Chocolate Crème Pudding Mix
1 egg yolk
½ tsp. vanilla
1 tsp. cornstarch

Place milk in mug and add Chocolate Crème Pudding Mix from bag. Mix well and heat in microwave until mixture begins to simmer, about 2 to 3 minutes. In a small bowl, combine egg yolk, vanilla and cornstarch. Add 2 tablespoons of the heated chocolate mixture to the egg yolk mixture. Stir well and return egg yolk mixture to mug with remaining chocolate mixture. Return to microwave for an additional minute. Cover and chill in refrigerator. Enjoy!

Chocolate Crème Pudding

- ¾ C. whole milk or half n' half
- Chocolate Crème Pudding Mix
- 1 egg yolk
- ½ tsp. vanilla
- 1 tsp. cornstarch

Place milk in mug and add Chocolate Crème Pudding Mix from bag. Mix well and heat in microwave until mixture begins to simmer, about 2 to 3 minutes. In a small bowl, combine egg yolk, vanilla and cornstarch. Add 2 tablespoons of the heated chocolate mixture to the egg yolk mixture. Stir well and return egg yolk mixture to mug with remaining chocolate mixture. Return to microwave for an additional minute. Cover and chill in refrigerator. Enjoy!

Chocolate Crème Pudding

- ¾ C. whole milk or half n' half
- Chocolate Crème Pudding Mix
- 1 egg yolk
- ½ tsp. vanilla
- 1 tsp. cornstarch

Place milk in mug and add Chocolate Crème Pudding Mix from bag. Mix well and heat in microwave until mixture begins to simmer, about 2 to 3 minutes. In a small bowl, combine egg yolk, vanilla and cornstarch. Add 2 tablespoons of the heated chocolate mixture to the egg yolk mixture. Stir well and return egg yolk mixture to mug with remaining chocolate mixture. Return to microwave for an additional minute. Cover and chill in refrigerator. Enjoy!

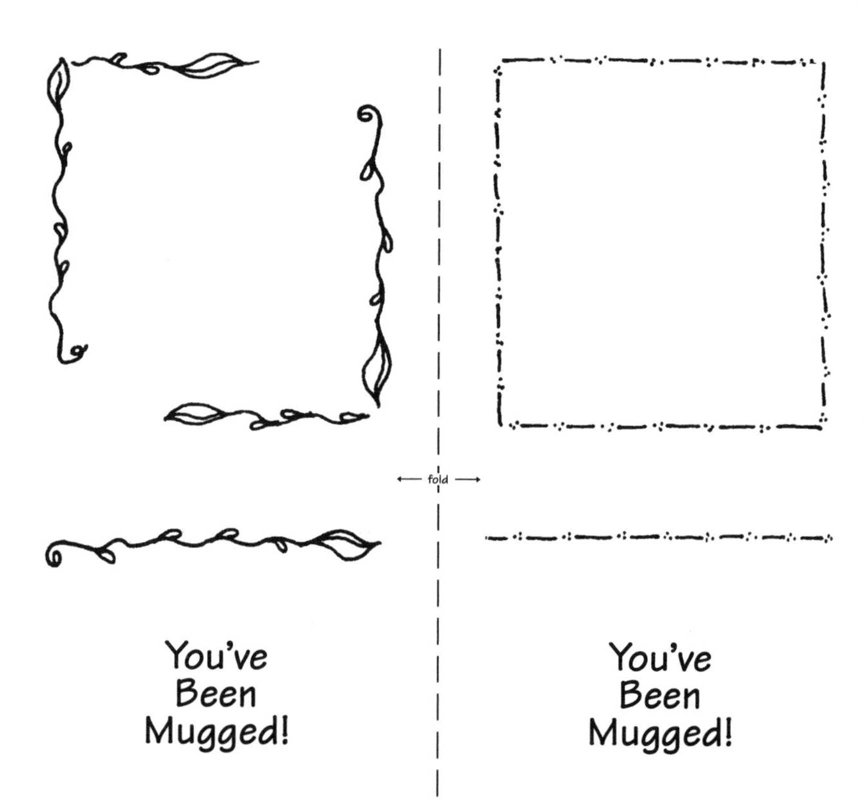
fold
You've
Been
Mugged!
MUG'EMS
by
CQ Products
www.cqproducts.com
You've
Been
Mugged!
MUG'EMS
by
CQ Products
www.cqproducts.com

Chocolate Crème Pudding

¾ C. whole milk
or half n' half
Chocolate Crème
Pudding Mix
1 egg yolk
½ tsp. vanilla
1 tsp. cornstarch

Place milk in mug and add Chocolate Crème Pudding Mix from bag. Mix well and heat in microwave until mixture begins to simmer, about 2 to 3 minutes. In a small bowl, combine egg yolk, vanilla and cornstarch. Add 2 tablespoons of the heated chocolate mixture to the egg yolk mixture. Stir well and return egg yolk mixture to mug with remaining chocolate mixture. Return to microwave for an additional minute. Cover and chill in refrigerator. Enjoy!

Chocolate Crème Pudding

¾ C. whole milk
or half n' half
Chocolate Crème
Pudding Mix
1 egg yolk
½ tsp. vanilla
1 tsp. cornstarch

Place milk in mug and add Chocolate Crème Pudding Mix from bag. Mix well and heat in microwave until mixture begins to simmer, about 2 to 3 minutes. In a small bowl, combine egg yolk, vanilla and cornstarch. Add 2 tablespoons of the heated chocolate mixture to the egg yolk mixture. Stir well and return egg yolk mixture to mug with remaining chocolate mixture. Return to microwave for an additional minute. Cover and chill in refrigerator. Enjoy!

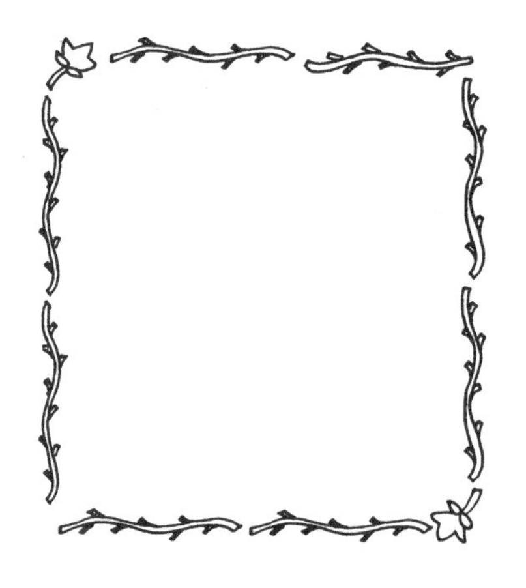

← fold →

You've
Been
Mugged!

MUG'EMS
by
CQ Products
www.cqproducts.com

You've
Been
Mugged!

MUG'EMS
by
CQ Products
www.cqproducts.com

Christmas Bread Pudding Mix

1½ T. raisins
1½ T. dried cherries or cranberries
1 C. dried, cubed bread
2½ T. sugar
¼ tsp. cinnamon
Pinch of nutmeg

In a small bowl, combine above ingredients. Mix well and place in a sandwich-size ziplock bag and seal. Place sealed bag in a mug. Make sure the mug holds a volume of at least 1½ cups.

Decorate mug and attach a gift tag with the directions on how to prepare the pudding.

Gift tag directions:
Christmas Bread Pudding

Christmas Bread Pudding Mix
1 T. butter
1 C. milk
1 egg yolk

Preheat oven to 325°. Lightly grease mug and add Christmas Bread Pudding Mix from bag. Mix until well incorporated. In a glass measuring cup, combine butter and milk. Microwave until butter is melted and stir in egg yolk. Pour heated milk mixture over ingredients in mug. Loosely cover mug with a small piece of aluminum foil. Bake in oven for 20 minutes. Let cool slightly. Enjoy!

Christmas Bread Pudding

Christmas Bread Pudding Mix
1 T. butter
1 C. milk
1 egg yolk

Preheat oven to 325°. Lightly grease mug and add Christmas Bread Pudding Mix from bag. Mix until well incorporated. In a glass measuring cup, combine butter and milk. Microwave until butter is melted and stir in egg yolk. Pour heated milk mixture over ingredients in mug. Loosely cover mug with a small piece of aluminum foil. Bake in oven for 20 minutes. Let cool slightly. Enjoy!

Christmas Bread Pudding

Christmas Bread Pudding Mix
1 T. butter
1 C. milk
1 egg yolk

Preheat oven to 325°. Lightly grease mug and add Christmas Bread Pudding Mix from bag. Mix until well incorporated. In a glass measuring cup, combine butter and milk. Microwave until butter is melted and stir in egg yolk. Pour heated milk mixture over ingredients in mug. Loosely cover mug with a small piece of aluminum foil. Bake in oven for 20 minutes. Let cool slightly. Enjoy!

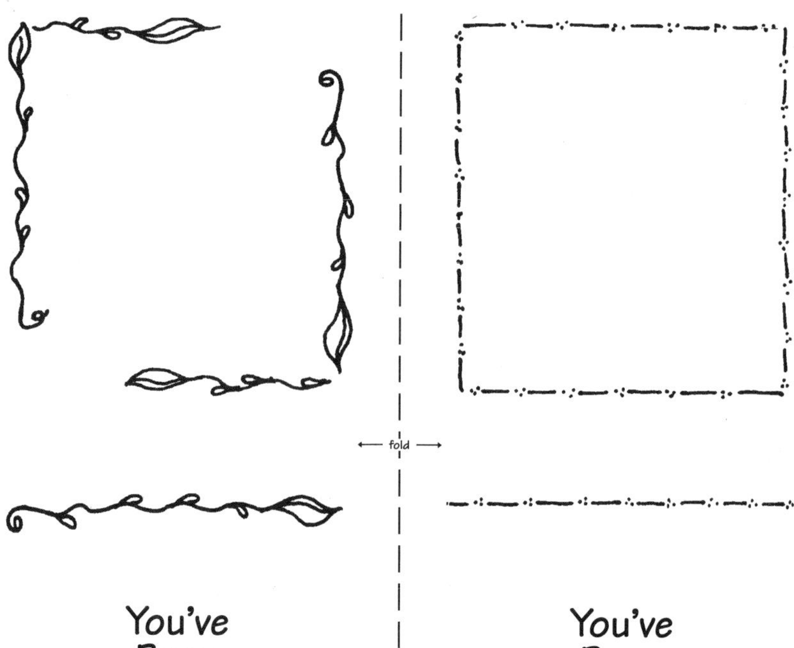

You've
Been
Mugged!

MUG'EMS
by
CQ Products
www.cqproducts.com

You've
Been
Mugged!

MUG'EMS
by
CQ Products
www.cqproducts.com

Christmas Bread Pudding

Christmas Bread Pudding Mix
1 T. butter
1 C. milk
1 egg yolk

Preheat oven to 325°. Lightly grease mug and add Christmas Bread Pudding Mix from bag. Mix until well incorporated. In a glass measuring cup, combine butter and milk. Microwave until butter is melted and stir in egg yolk. Pour heated milk mixture over ingredients in mug. Loosely cover mug with a small piece of aluminum foil. Bake in oven for 20 minutes. Let cool slightly. Enjoy!

Christmas Bread Pudding

Christmas Bread Pudding Mix
1 T. butter
1 C. milk
1 egg yolk

Preheat oven to 325°. Lightly grease mug and add Christmas Bread Pudding Mix from bag. Mix until well incorporated. In a glass measuring cup, combine butter and milk. Microwave until butter is melted and stir in egg yolk. Pour heated milk mixture over ingredients in mug. Loosely cover mug with a small piece of aluminum foil. Bake in oven for 20 minutes. Let cool slightly. Enjoy!

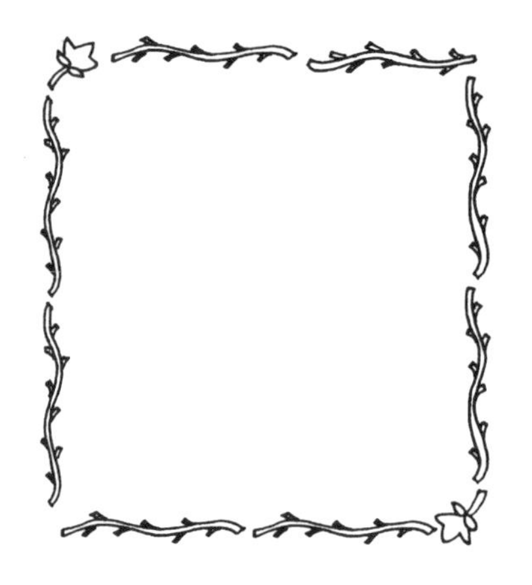

← fold →

You've
Been
Mugged!

MUG'EMS
by
CQ Products
www.cqproducts.com

You've
Been
Mugged!

MUG'EMS
by
CQ Products
www.cqproducts.com

Pumpkin Pie Mix

4 T. graham cracker crumbs
3½ T. sugar, divided
½ tsp. cinnamon, divided
Pinch of nutmeg
Pinch of ground cloves
Pinch of allspice

In a small bowl, combine graham cracker crumbs, ½ tablespoon sugar and ¼ teaspoon cinnamon. Mix well and place in a small ziplock bag and seal. Place sealed bag in a mug. Make sure the mug holds a volume of at least 1½ cups. In a separate ziplock bag, place remaining 3 tablespoons sugar, remaining ¼ teaspoon cinnamon, nutmeg, ground cloves and allspice. Place bag inside mug with other bag.

Decorate mug and attach a gift tag with the directions on how to prepare the pie.

Gift tag directions: Pumpkin Pie

2 T. butter, melted
Pumpkin Pie Mix
1 egg yolk
½ C. pumpkin puree
½ C. whole milk

Preheat oven to 350°. To make crust, in a small bowl, combine melted butter and contents of bag containing graham cracker crumbs. Mix well and press mixture into the bottom and halfway up sides of lightly greased mug. Bake in oven for 6 to 8 minutes. Meanwhile, in a separate bowl, combine contents of remaining bag, egg yolk, pumpkin puree and whole milk. Mix for 1 minute, until smooth. Allow crust to cool slightly and pour pumpkin mixture over crust in mug. Bake in oven for 20 to 25 minutes. Enjoy!

Pumpkin Pie

2 T. butter, melted
Pumpkin Pie Mix
1 egg yolk
½ C. pumpkin puree
½ C. whole milk

Preheat oven to 350°. To make crust, in a small bowl, combine melted butter and contents of bag containing graham cracker crumbs. Mix well and press mixture into the bottom and halfway up sides of lightly greased mug. Bake in oven for 6 to 8 minutes. Meanwhile, in a separate bowl, combine contents of remaining bag, egg yolk, pumpkin puree and whole milk. Mix for 1 minute, until smooth. Allow crust to cool slightly and pour pumpkin mixture over crust in mug. Bake in oven for 20 to 25 minutes. Enjoy!

Pumpkin Pie

2 T. butter, melted
Pumpkin Pie Mix
1 egg yolk
½ C. pumpkin puree
½ C. whole milk

Preheat oven to 350°. To make crust, in a small bowl, combine melted butter and contents of bag containing graham cracker crumbs. Mix well and press mixture into the bottom and halfway up sides of lightly greased mug. Bake in oven for 6 to 8 minutes. Meanwhile, in a separate bowl, combine contents of remaining bag, egg yolk, pumpkin puree and whole milk. Mix for 1 minute, until smooth. Allow crust to cool slightly and pour pumpkin mixture over crust in mug. Bake in oven for 20 to 25 minutes. Enjoy!

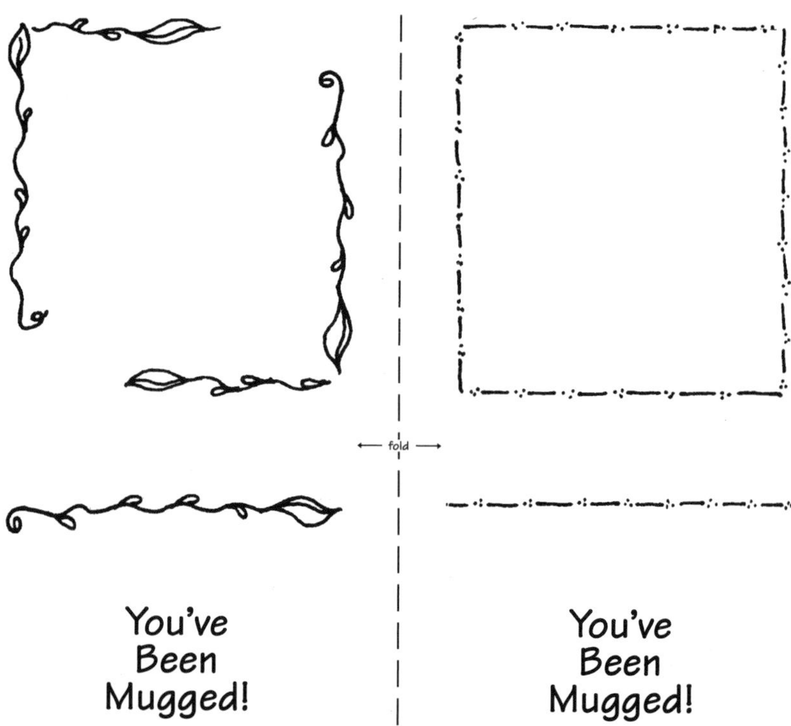

MUG'EMS
by
CQ Products
www.cqproducts.com

MUG'EMS
by
CQ Products
www.cqproducts.com

Pumpkin Pie

2 T. butter, melted
Pumpkin Pie Mix
1 egg yolk
½ C. pumpkin puree
½ C. whole milk

Preheat oven to 350°. To make crust, in a small bowl, combine melted butter and contents of bag containing graham cracker crumbs. Mix well and press mixture into the bottom and halfway up sides of lightly greased mug. Bake in oven for 6 to 8 minutes. Meanwhile, in a separate bowl, combine contents of remaining bag, egg yolk, pumpkin puree and whole milk. Mix for 1 minute, until smooth. Allow crust to cool slightly and pour pumpkin mixture over crust in mug. Bake in oven for 20 to 25 minutes. Enjoy!

Pumpkin Pie

2 T. butter, melted
Pumpkin Pie Mix
1 egg yolk
½ C. pumpkin puree
½ C. whole milk

Preheat oven to 350°. To make crust, in a small bowl, combine melted butter and contents of bag containing graham cracker crumbs. Mix well and press mixture into the bottom and halfway up sides of lightly greased mug. Bake in oven for 6 to 8 minutes. Meanwhile, in a separate bowl, combine contents of remaining bag, egg yolk, pumpkin puree and whole milk. Mix for 1 minute, until smooth. Allow crust to cool slightly and pour pumpkin mixture over crust in mug. Bake in oven for 20 to 25 minutes. Enjoy!

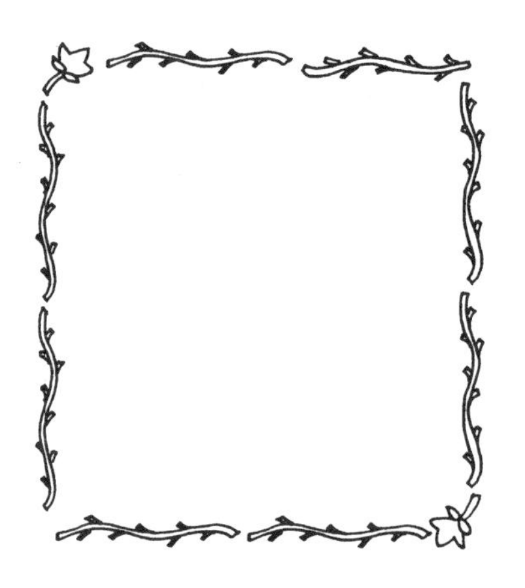

← fold →

You've
Been
Mugged!

MUG'EMS
by
CQ Products
www.cqproducts.com

You've
Been
Mugged!

MUG'EMS
by
CQ Products
www.cqproducts.com

Corn Bread Stuffing Mix

1 C. dried, crumbled corn bread
1½ T. chopped pecans
½ tsp. dried onion flakes
1 tsp. celery flakes
1 tsp. chicken bouillon
½ T. craisins

In a small bowl, combine above ingredients. Mix well and place in a sandwich-size ziplock bag and seal. Place sealed bag in a mug. Make sure the mug holds a volume of at least 1½ cups.

Decorate mug and attach a gift tag with the directions on how to prepare the stuffing.

Gift tag directions: Corn Bread Stuffing

Corn Bread Stuffing Mix
1½ T. butter
½ C. water

Preheat oven to 350°. In a small bowl, place Corn Bread Stuffing Mix from bag. In a glass measuring cup, combine butter and water. Heat in microwave until butter is melted. Pour melted butter mixture over ingredients in bowl and toss until evenly incorporated. Place mixture in lightly greased mug. Loosely cover mug with a small piece of aluminum foil. Bake in oven for 20 minutes. Let cool slightly. Enjoy!

Corn Bread Stuffing

Corn Bread Stuffing Mix
1½ T. butter
½ C. water

Preheat oven to 350°. In a small bowl, place Corn Bread Stuffing Mix from bag. In a glass measuring cup, combine butter and water. Heat in microwave until butter is melted. Pour melted butter mixture over ingredients in bowl and toss until evenly incorporated. Place mixture in lightly greased mug. Loosely cover mug with a small piece of aluminum foil. Bake in oven for 20 minutes. Let cool slightly. Enjoy!

Corn Bread Stuffing

Corn Bread Stuffing Mix
1½ T. butter
½ C. water

Preheat oven to 350°. In a small bowl, place Corn Bread Stuffing Mix from bag. In a glass measuring cup, combine butter and water. Heat in microwave until butter is melted. Pour melted butter mixture over ingredients in bowl and toss until evenly incorporated. Place mixture in lightly greased mug. Loosely cover mug with a small piece of aluminum foil. Bake in oven for 20 minutes. Let cool slightly. Enjoy!

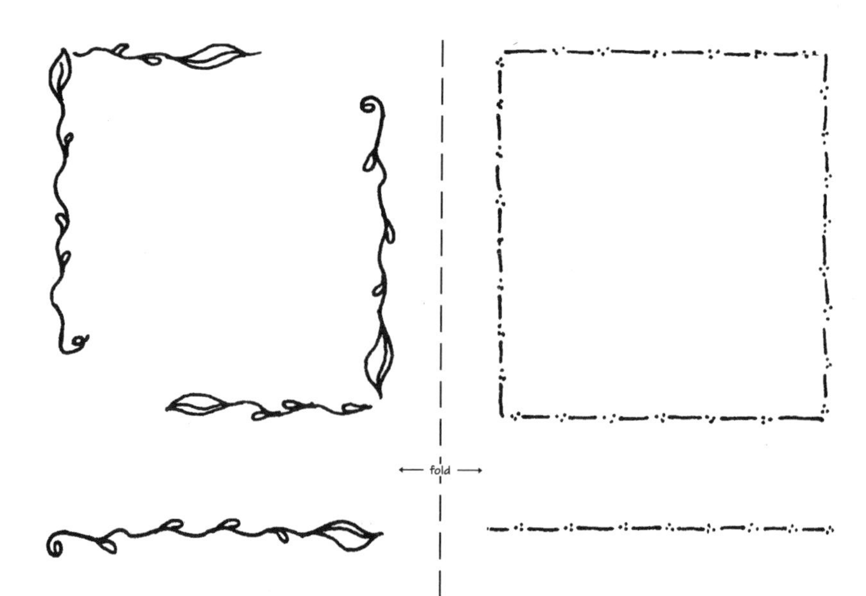

You've
Been
Mugged!

MUG'EMS
by
CQ Products
www.cqproducts.com

You've
Been
Mugged!

MUG'EMS
by
CQ Products
www.cqproducts.com

Corn Bread Stuffing

Corn Bread Stuffing Mix
1½ T. butter
½ C. water

Preheat oven to 350°. In a small bowl, place Corn Bread Stuffing Mix from bag. In a glass measuring cup, combine butter and water. Heat in microwave until butter is melted. Pour melted butter mixture over ingredients in bowl and toss until evenly incorporated. Place mixture in lightly greased mug. Loosely cover mug with a small piece of aluminum foil. Bake in oven for 20 minutes. Let cool slightly. Enjoy!

Corn Bread Stuffing

Corn Bread Stuffing Mix
1½ T. butter
½ C. water

Preheat oven to 350°. In a small bowl, place Corn Bread Stuffing Mix from bag. In a glass measuring cup, combine butter and water. Heat in microwave until butter is melted. Pour melted butter mixture over ingredients in bowl and toss until evenly incorporated. Place mixture in lightly greased mug. Loosely cover mug with a small piece of aluminum foil. Bake in oven for 20 minutes. Let cool slightly. Enjoy!

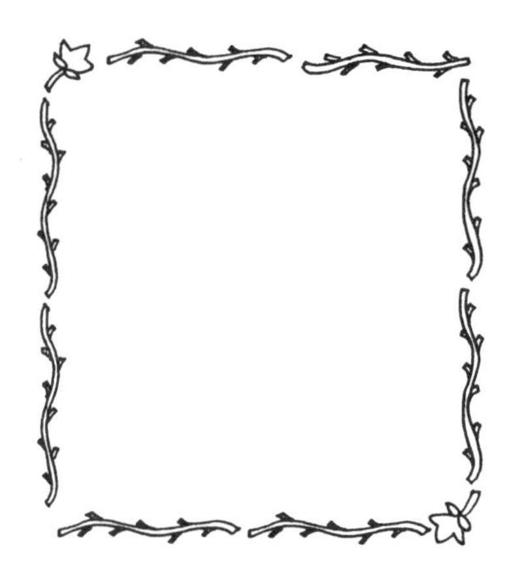

← fold →

You've
Been
Mugged!

You've
Been
Mugged!

MUG'EMS
by
CQ Products
www.cqproducts.com

Sweet Potato Pudding Mix

1½ T. raisins or dates
1 T. sugar
1½ T. dark brown sugar
¼ tsp. cinnamon
Pinch of nutmeg
Pinch of salt

In a small bowl, combine above ingredients. Mix well and place in a sandwich-size ziplock bag and seal. Place sealed bag in a mug. Make sure the mug holds a volume of at least 1½ cups.

Decorate mug and attach a gift tag with the directions on how to prepare the pudding.

Gift tag directions: Sweet Potato Pudding

1 T. butter, melted
1 small egg
½ C. fresh or canned mashed sweet potato
½ C. evaporated milk
Sweet Potato Pudding Mix

Preheat oven to 350°. In a small bowl, combine melted butter, egg, mashed sweet potato, evaporated milk and Sweet Potato Pudding Mix from bag. Mix well, until sugar and brown sugar are completely dissolved. Pour mixture into lightly greased mug. Place mug in a pot. Fill pot with water until water level is halfway up side of mug. Place pot with mug in oven and bake for 30 minutes. Enjoy!

Sweet Potato Pudding

1 T. butter, melted
1 small egg
½ C. fresh or canned mashed sweet potato
½ C. evaporated milk
Sweet Potato Pudding Mix

Preheat oven to 350°. In a small bowl, combine melted butter, egg, mashed sweet potato, evaporated milk and Sweet Potato Pudding Mix from bag. Mix well, until sugar and brown sugar are completely dissolved. Pour mixture into lightly greased mug. Place mug in a pot. Fill pot with water until water level is halfway up side of mug. Place pot with mug in oven and bake for 30 minutes. Enjoy!

Sweet Potato Pudding

1 T. butter, melted
1 small egg
½ C. fresh or canned mashed sweet potato
½ C. evaporated milk
Sweet Potato Pudding Mix

Preheat oven to 350°. In a small bowl, combine melted butter, egg, mashed sweet potato, evaporated milk and Sweet Potato Pudding Mix from bag. Mix well, until sugar and brown sugar are completely dissolved. Pour mixture into lightly greased mug. Place mug in a pot. Fill pot with water until water level is halfway up side of mug. Place pot with mug in oven and bake for 30 minutes. Enjoy!

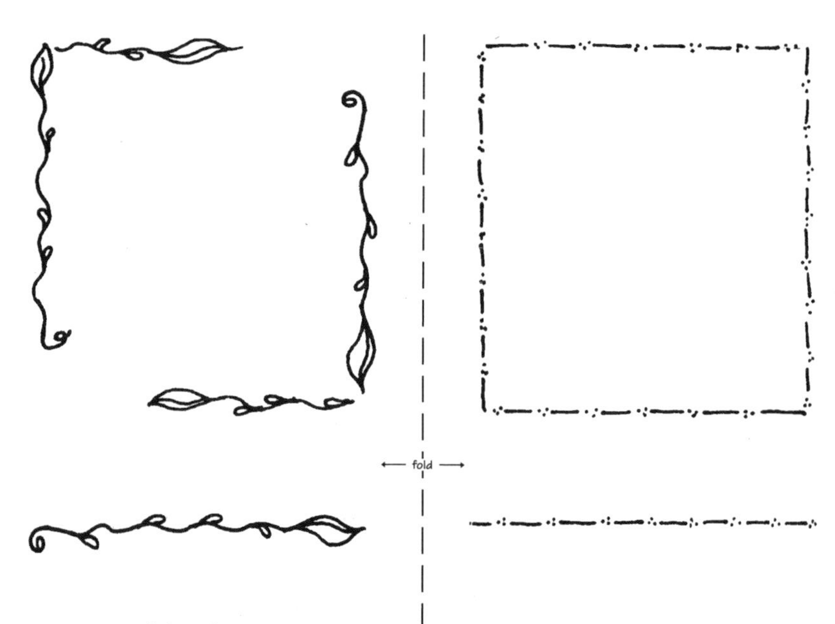

You've
Been
Mugged!

MUG'EMS
by
CQ Products
www.cqproducts.com

You've
Been
Mugged!

MUG'EMS
by
CQ Products
www.cqproducts.com

Sweet Potato Pudding

1 T. butter, melted
1 small egg
½ C. fresh or canned mashed sweet potato
½ C. evaporated milk
Sweet Potato Pudding Mix

Preheat oven to 350°. In a small bowl, combine melted butter, egg, mashed sweet potato, evaporated milk and Sweet Potato Pudding Mix from bag. Mix well, until sugar and brown sugar are completely dissolved. Pour mixture into lightly greased mug. Place mug in a pot. Fill pot with water until water level is halfway up side of mug. Place pot with mug in oven and bake for 30 minutes. Enjoy!

Sweet Potato Pudding

1 T. butter, melted
1 small egg
½ C. fresh or canned mashed sweet potato
½ C. evaporated milk
Sweet Potato Pudding Mix

Preheat oven to 350°. In a small bowl, combine melted butter, egg, mashed sweet potato, evaporated milk and Sweet Potato Pudding Mix from bag. Mix well, until sugar and brown sugar are completely dissolved. Pour mixture into lightly greased mug. Place mug in a pot. Fill pot with water until water level is halfway up side of mug. Place pot with mug in oven and bake for 30 minutes. Enjoy!

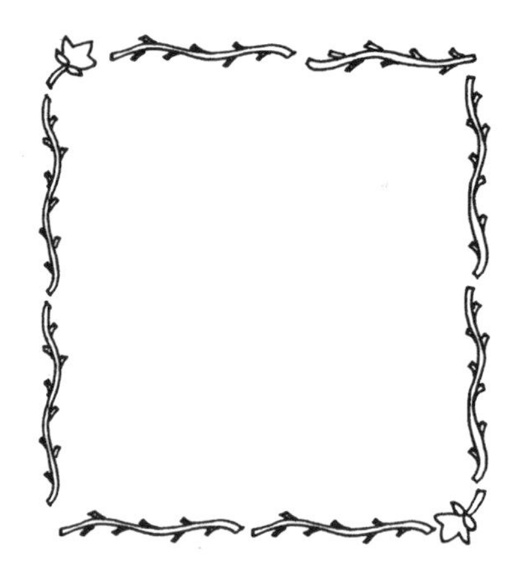

← fold →

You've
Been
Mugged!

MUG'EMS
by
CQ Products
www.cqproducts.com

You've
Been
Mugged!

MUG'EMS
by
CQ Products
www.cqproducts.com

Christmas Custard Mix

⅓ C. crumbled macaroon cookies
2 T. chopped mixed candied fruit
2 T. chopped raisins
2 T. sugar

In a small bowl, combine above ingredients. Mix well and place in a sandwich-size ziplock bag and seal. Place sealed bag in a mug. Make sure the mug holds a volume of at least 1½ cups.

Decorate mug and attach a gift tag with the directions on how to prepare the custard.

Gift tag directions:
Christmas Custard

1 small egg
2/3 C. whole milk
1/4 tsp. vanilla or rum extract
Christmas Custard Mix

Preheat oven to 325°. In a small bowl, combine egg, milk, vanilla and Christmas Custard Mix from bag. Let mixture sit for a few minutes. Pour mixture into lightly greased mug. Place mug in a pot. Fill pot with water until water level is halfway up side of mug. Place pot with mug in oven and bake for 30 minutes. Enjoy!

Christmas Custard

1 small egg
2/3 C. whole milk
1/4 tsp. vanilla or rum extract
Christmas Custard Mix

Preheat oven to 325°. In a small bowl, combine egg, milk, vanilla and Christmas Custard Mix from bag. Let mixture sit for a few minutes. Pour mixture into lightly greased mug. Place mug in a pot. Fill pot with water until water level is halfway up side of mug. Place pot with mug in oven and bake for 30 minutes. Enjoy!

Christmas Custard

1 small egg
2/3 C. whole milk
1/4 tsp. vanilla or rum extract
Christmas Custard Mix

Preheat oven to 325°. In a small bowl, combine egg, milk, vanilla and Christmas Custard Mix from bag. Let mixture sit for a few minutes. Pour mixture into lightly greased mug. Place mug in a pot. Fill pot with water until water level is halfway up side of mug. Place pot with mug in oven and bake for 30 minutes. Enjoy!

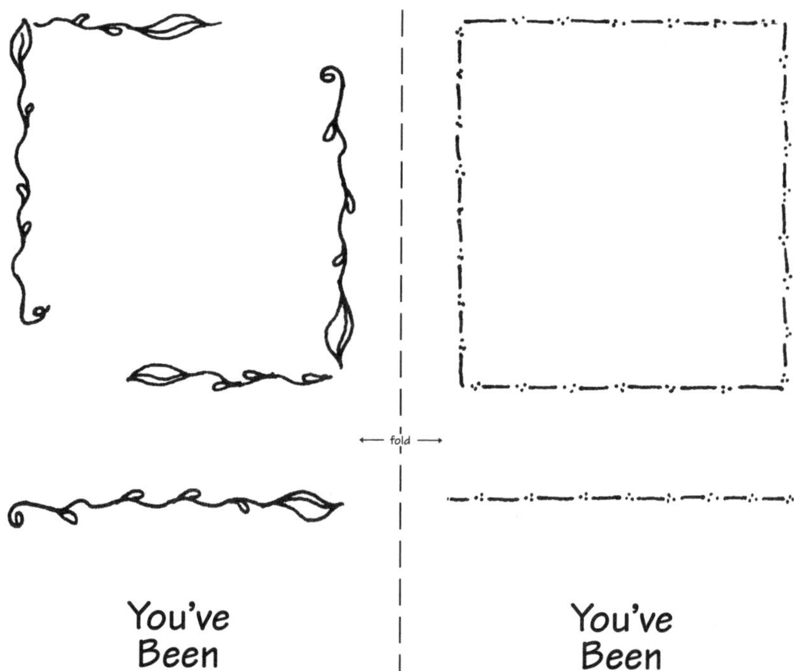

You've
Been
Mugged!

MUG'EMS
by
CQ Products
www.cqproducts.com

You've
Been
Mugged!

MUG'EMS
by
CQ Products
www.cqproducts.com

Christmas Custard

1 small egg
2/3 C. whole milk
1/4 tsp. vanilla or
rum extract
Christmas Custard Mix

Preheat oven to 325°. In a small bowl, combine egg, milk, vanilla and Christmas Custard Mix from bag. Let mixture sit for a few minutes. Pour mixture into lightly greased mug. Place mug in a pot. Fill pot with water until water level is halfway up side of mug. Place pot with mug in oven and bake for 30 minutes. Enjoy!

Christmas Custard

1 small egg
2/3 C. whole milk
1/4 tsp. vanilla or
rum extract
Christmas Custard Mix

Preheat oven to 325°. In a small bowl, combine egg, milk, vanilla and Christmas Custard Mix from bag. Let mixture sit for a few minutes. Pour mixture into lightly greased mug. Place mug in a pot. Fill pot with water until water level is halfway up side of mug. Place pot with mug in oven and bake for 30 minutes. Enjoy!

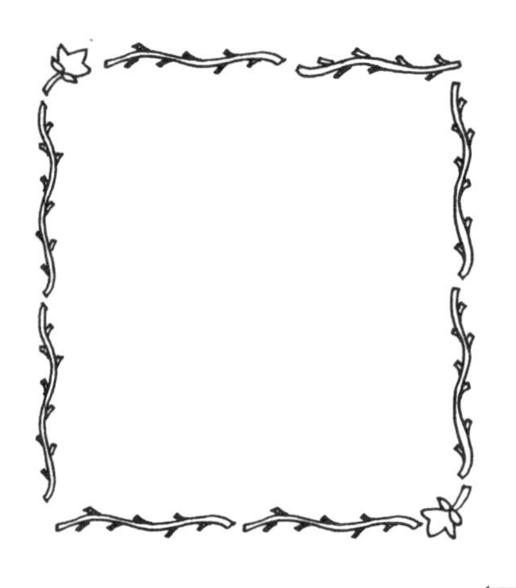

← fold →

You've
Been
Mugged!

MUG'EMS
by
CQ Products
www.cqproducts.com

You've
Been
Mugged!

MUG'EMS
by
CQ Products
www.cqproducts.com

Sweet Potato Apple Bake Mix

2 T. dried apples
1 T. raisins
¼ tsp. cinnamon
2 tsp. sugar
1 tsp. dried parsley flakes
1 tsp. chicken bouillon

In a small bowl, combine above ingredients. Mix well and place in a sandwich-size ziplock bag and seal. Place sealed bag in a mug. Make sure the mug holds a volume of at least 1½ cups.

Decorate mug and attach a gift tag with the directions on how to prepare the dessert.

Gift tag directions:
Sweet Potato Apple Bake

2 T. butter, melted
2 T. water
1 C. peeled and cubed sweet potatoes
Sweet Potato Apple Bake Mix

Preheat oven to 350°. In a small bowl, combine melted butter and water. Add peeled and cubed sweet potatoes and Sweet Potato Apple Bake Mix from bag. Mix well and place mixture in lightly greased mug. Loosely cover mug with a small piece of aluminum foil. Bake in oven for 22 to 24 minutes. Enjoy!

Sweet Potato Apple Bake

2 T. butter, melted
2 T. water
1 C. peeled and cubed sweet potatoes
Sweet Potato Apple Bake Mix

Preheat oven to 350°. In a small bowl, combine melted butter and water. Add peeled and cubed sweet potatoes and Sweet Potato Apple Bake Mix from bag. Mix well and place mixture in lightly greased mug. Loosely cover mug with a small piece of aluminum foil. Bake in oven for 22 to 24 minutes. Enjoy!

Sweet Potato Apple Bake

2 T. butter, melted
2 T. water
1 C. peeled and cubed sweet potatoes
Sweet Potato Apple Bake Mix

Preheat oven to 350°. In a small bowl, combine melted butter and water. Add peeled and cubed sweet potatoes and Sweet Potato Apple Bake Mix from bag. Mix well and place mixture in lightly greased mug. Loosely cover mug with a small piece of aluminum foil. Bake in oven for 22 to 24 minutes. Enjoy!

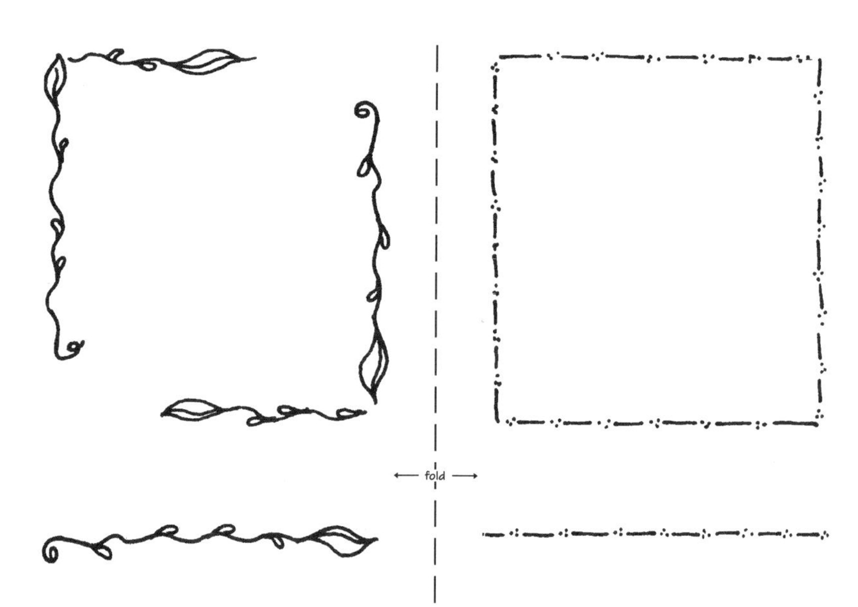

You've
Been
Mugged!

MUG'EMS
by
CQ Products
www.cqproducts.com

You've
Been
Mugged!

MUG'EMS
by
CQ Products
www.cqproducts.com

Sweet Potato Apple Bake

2 T. butter, melted
2 T. water
1 C. peeled and cubed sweet potatoes
Sweet Potato Apple Bake Mix

Preheat oven to 350°. In a small bowl, combine melted butter and water. Add peeled and cubed sweet potatoes and Sweet Potato Apple Bake Mix from bag. Mix well and place mixture in lightly greased mug. Loosely cover mug with a small piece of aluminum foil. Bake in oven for 22 to 24 minutes. Enjoy!

Sweet Potato Apple Bake

2 T. butter, melted
2 T. water
1 C. peeled and cubed sweet potatoes
Sweet Potato Apple Bake Mix

Preheat oven to 350°. In a small bowl, combine melted butter and water. Add peeled and cubed sweet potatoes and Sweet Potato Apple Bake Mix from bag. Mix well and place mixture in lightly greased mug. Loosely cover mug with a small piece of aluminum foil. Bake in oven for 22 to 24 minutes. Enjoy!

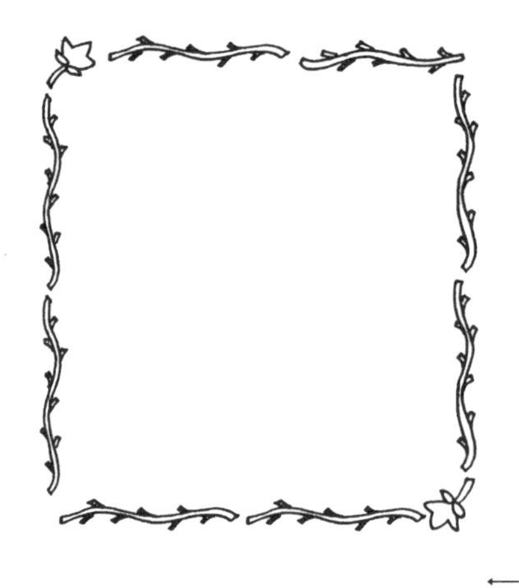

← fold →

You've
Been
Mugged!

MUG'EMS
by
CQ Products
www.cqproducts.com

You've
Been
Mugged!

MUG'EMS
by
CQ Products
www.cqproducts.com

Cherry Brownie Pudding Cake Mix

⅓ C. flour
3 T. sugar
¾ tsp. baking powder
Pinch of salt
2 T. miniature chocolate chips
1½ T. instant fudge pudding mix

In a small bowl, combine above ingredients. Mix well and place in a sandwich-size ziplock bag and seal. Place sealed bag in a mug. Make sure the mug holds a volume of at least 1½ cups.

Decorate mug and attach a gift tag with the directions on how to prepare the dessert.

Gift tag directions:
Cherry Brownie Pudding Cake

2½ T. shortening
Cherry Brownie Pudding Cake Mix
¼ C. milk
1 small egg
½ tsp. vanilla
1 (1 oz.) square semisweet chocolate, melted
2 T. cherry pie filling
Whipped cream, optional

Preheat oven to 350°. In a small bowl, combine shortening and Cherry Brownie Pudding Cake Mix from bag. Add milk, egg and vanilla and stir for 1 minute, until smooth. Stir in melted chocolate and mix until blended. Place cherry pie filling in the bottom of lightly greased mug. Pour chocolate batter over cherry filling. Bake in oven for 18 to 22 minutes. If desired, add a dollop of whipped cream. Enjoy!

Cherry Brownie Pudding Cake

2½ T. shortening
Cherry Brownie Pudding Cake Mix
¼ C. milk
1 small egg
½ tsp. vanilla
1 (1 oz.) square semisweet chocolate, melted
2 T. cherry pie filling
Whipped cream, optional

Preheat oven to 350°. In a small bowl, combine shortening and Cherry Brownie Pudding Cake Mix from bag. Add milk, egg and vanilla and stir for 1 minute, until smooth. Stir in melted chocolate and mix until blended. Place cherry pie filling in the bottom of lightly greased mug. Pour chocolate batter over cherry filling. Bake in oven for 18 to 22 minutes. If desired, add a dollop of whipped cream. Enjoy!

Cherry Brownie Pudding Cake

2½ T. shortening
Cherry Brownie Pudding Cake Mix
¼ C. milk
1 small egg
½ tsp. vanilla
1 (1 oz.) square semisweet chocolate, melted
2 T. cherry pie filling
Whipped cream, optional

Preheat oven to 350°. In a small bowl, combine shortening and Cherry Brownie Pudding Cake Mix from bag. Add milk, egg and vanilla and stir for 1 minute, until smooth. Stir in melted chocolate and mix until blended. Place cherry pie filling in the bottom of lightly greased mug. Pour chocolate batter over cherry filling. Bake in oven for 18 to 22 minutes. If desired, add a dollop of whipped cream. Enjoy!

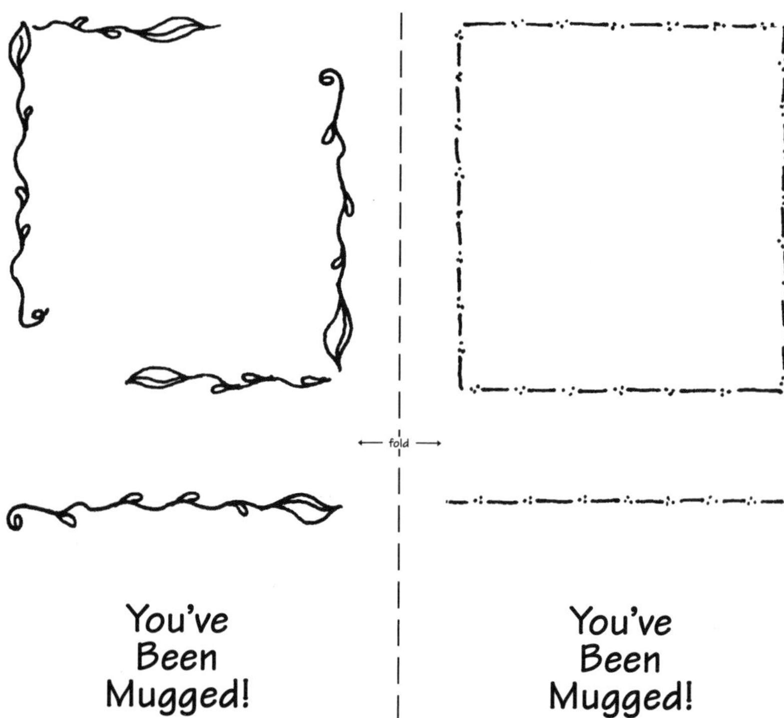

MUG'EMS
by
CQ Products
www.cqproducts.com

MUG'EMS
by
CQ Products
www.cqproducts.com

Cherry Brownie Pudding Cake

2½ T. shortening
Cherry Brownie Pudding Cake Mix
¼ C. milk
1 small egg
½ tsp. vanilla
1 (1 oz.) square semisweet chocolate, melted
2 T. cherry pie filling
Whipped cream, optional

Preheat oven to 350°. In a small bowl, combine shortening and Cherry Brownie Pudding Cake Mix from bag. Add milk, egg and vanilla and stir for 1 minute, until smooth. Stir in melted chocolate and mix until blended. Place cherry pie filling in the bottom of lightly greased mug. Pour chocolate batter over cherry filling. Bake in oven for 18 to 22 minutes. If desired, add a dollop of whipped cream. Enjoy!

Cherry Brownie Pudding Cake

2½ T. shortening
Cherry Brownie Pudding Cake Mix
¼ C. milk
1 small egg
½ tsp. vanilla
1 (1 oz.) square semisweet chocolate, melted
2 T. cherry pie filling
Whipped cream, optional

Preheat oven to 350°. In a small bowl, combine shortening and Cherry Brownie Pudding Cake Mix from bag. Add milk, egg and vanilla and stir for 1 minute, until smooth. Stir in melted chocolate and mix until blended. Place cherry pie filling in the bottom of lightly greased mug. Pour chocolate batter over cherry filling. Bake in oven for 18 to 22 minutes. If desired, add a dollop of whipped cream. Enjoy!

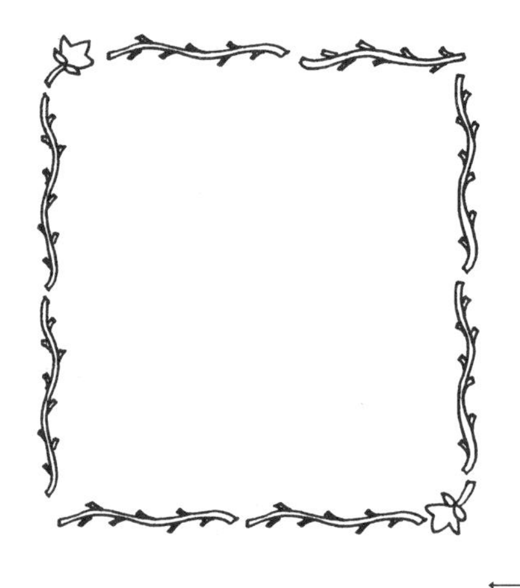

← fold →

You've
Been
Mugged!

MUG'EMS
by
CQ Products
www.cqproducts.com

You've
Been
Mugged!

MUG'EMS
by
CQ Products
www.cqproducts.com

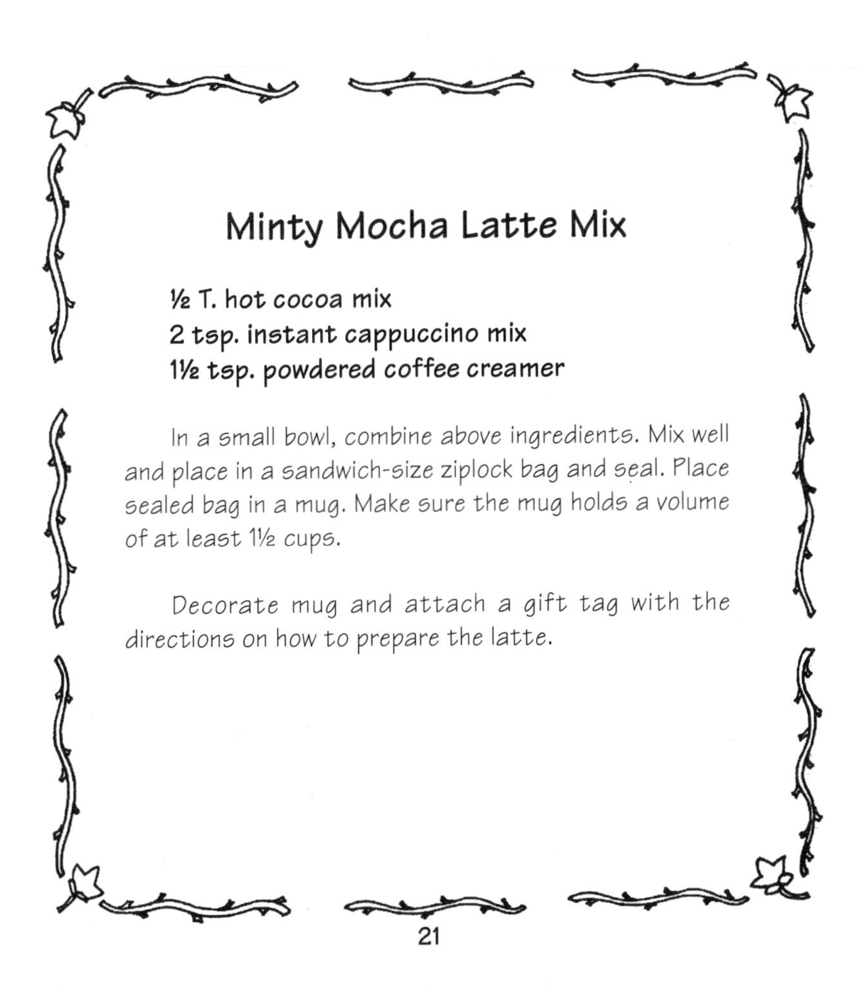

Minty Mocha Latte Mix

½ T. hot cocoa mix
2 tsp. instant cappuccino mix
1½ tsp. powdered coffee creamer

In a small bowl, combine above ingredients. Mix well and place in a sandwich-size ziplock bag and seal. Place sealed bag in a mug. Make sure the mug holds a volume of at least 1½ cups.

Decorate mug and attach a gift tag with the directions on how to prepare the latte.

Gift tag directions: Minty Mocha Latte

8 oz. water
Minty Mocha Latte Mix
1 T. Crème de Menthe liqueur
Whipped cream

In a small saucepan over medium heat, place water. Bring water to a low simmer. Place Minty Mocha Latte Mix from bag in mug. Pour hot water over ingredients in mug and stir until completely dissolved. Stir in Crème de Menthe and top with a dollop of whipped cream. Enjoy!

Minty Mocha Latte

8 oz. water
Minty Mocha Latte Mix
1 T. Crème de Menthe liqueur
Whipped cream

In a small saucepan over medium heat, place water. Bring water to a low simmer. Place Minty Mocha Latte Mix from bag in mug. Pour hot water over ingredients in mug and stir until completely dissolved. Stir in Crème de Menthe and top with a dollop of whipped cream. Enjoy!

Minty Mocha Latte

8 oz. water
Minty Mocha Latte Mix
1 T. Crème de Menthe liqueur
Whipped cream

In a small saucepan over medium heat, place water. Bring water to a low simmer. Place Minty Mocha Latte Mix from bag in mug. Pour hot water over ingredients in mug and stir until completely dissolved. Stir in Crème de Menthe and top with a dollop of whipped cream. Enjoy!

fold
You've
Been
Mugged!
MUG'EMS
by
CQ Products
www.cqproducts.com
You've
Been
Mugged!
MUG'EMS
by
CQ Products
www.cqproducts.com

Minty Mocha Latte

8 oz. water
Minty Mocha Latte Mix
1 T. Crème de Menthe liqueur
Whipped cream

In a small saucepan over medium heat, place water. Bring water to a low simmer. Place Minty Mocha Latte Mix from bag in mug. Pour hot water over ingredients in mug and stir until completely dissolved. Stir in Crème de Menthe and top with a dollop of whipped cream. Enjoy!

Minty Mocha Latte

8 oz. water
Minty Mocha Latte Mix
1 T. Crème de Menthe liqueur
Whipped cream

In a small saucepan over medium heat, place water. Bring water to a low simmer. Place Minty Mocha Latte Mix from bag in mug. Pour hot water over ingredients in mug and stir until completely dissolved. Stir in Crème de Menthe and top with a dollop of whipped cream. Enjoy!

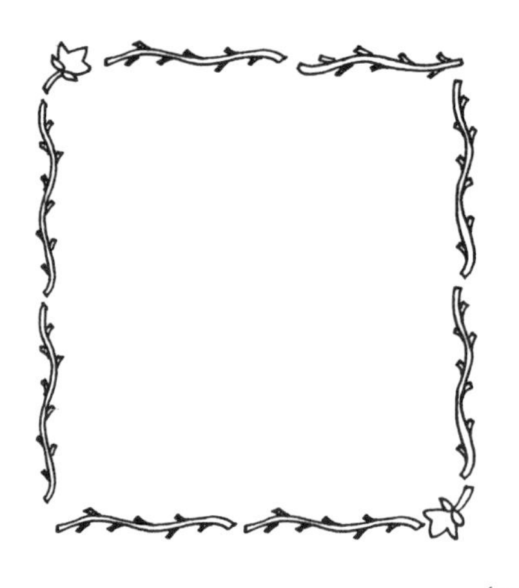

← fold →

You've
Been
Mugged!

MUG'EMS
by
CQ Products
www.cqproducts.com

You've
Been
Mugged!

MUG'EMS
by
CQ Products
www.cqproducts.com

Apple Cranberry Crisp Mix

3 T. flour, divided
3 T. old fashioned oats
¼ tsp. cinnamon
1 T. finely chopped walnuts or pecans
2 T. brown sugar
2½ T. sugar

In a small bowl, combine 2 tablespoons flour, old fashioned oats, cinnamon, chopped walnuts and brown sugar. Mix well and place in a small ziplock bag and seal. Place sealed bag in a mug. Make sure the mug holds a volume of at least 1½ cups. In a separate ziplock bag, place remaining 1 tablespoon flour and sugar. Place bag inside mug with other bag.

Decorate mug and attach a gift tag with the directions on how to prepare the crisp.

Gift tag directions: Apple Cranberry Crisp

1 medium apple
¼ C. fresh cranberries
Apple Cranberry Crisp Mix
3 T. butter or margarine, softened

Preheat oven to 350°. Peel, core and chop apple. Place chopped apple in a small bowl. Coarsely chop cranberries and add to chopped apples. Add contents of bag containing only sugar and flour. Mix well and place mixture in lightly greased mug. In a separate bowl, combine contents of remaining bag. Using a pastry blender, cut in butter until mixture resembles fine crumbs. Place crumb mixture over apple mixture in mug. Bake in oven for 20 minutes. Enjoy!

Apple Cranberry Crisp

1 medium apple
¼ C. fresh cranberries
Apple Cranberry Crisp Mix
3 T. butter or margarine, softened

Preheat oven to 350°. Peel, core and chop apple. Place chopped apple in a small bowl. Coarsely chop cranberries and add to chopped apples. Add contents of bag containing only sugar and flour. Mix well and place mixture in lightly greased mug. In a separate bowl, combine contents of remaining bag. Using a pastry blender, cut in butter until mixture resembles fine crumbs. Place crumb mixture over apple mixture in mug. Bake in oven for 20 minutes. Enjoy!

Apple Cranberry Crisp

1 medium apple
¼ C. fresh cranberries
Apple Cranberry Crisp Mix
3 T. butter or margarine, softened

Preheat oven to 350°. Peel, core and chop apple. Place chopped apple in a small bowl. Coarsely chop cranberries and add to chopped apples. Add contents of bag containing only sugar and flour. Mix well and place mixture in lightly greased mug. In a separate bowl, combine contents of remaining bag. Using a pastry blender, cut in butter until mixture resembles fine crumbs. Place crumb mixture over apple mixture in mug. Bake in oven for 20 minutes. Enjoy!

fold
You've
Been
Mugged!
MUG'EMS
by
CQ Products
www.cqproducts.com
You've
Been
Mugged!
MUG'EMS
by
CQ Products
www.cqproducts.com

Apple Cranberry Crisp

1 medium apple
¼ C. fresh cranberries
Apple Cranberry Crisp Mix
3 T. butter or margarine, softened

Preheat oven to 350°. Peel, core and chop apple. Place chopped apple in a small bowl. Coarsely chop cranberries and add to chopped apples. Add contents of bag containing only sugar and flour. Mix well and place mixture in lightly greased mug. In a separate bowl, combine contents of remaining bag. Using a pastry blender, cut in butter until mixture resembles fine crumbs. Place crumb mixture over apple mixture in mug. Bake in oven for 20 minutes. Enjoy!

Apple Cranberry Crisp

1 medium apple
¼ C. fresh cranberries
Apple Cranberry Crisp Mix
3 T. butter or margarine, softened

Preheat oven to 350°. Peel, core and chop apple. Place chopped apple in a small bowl. Coarsely chop cranberries and add to chopped apples. Add contents of bag containing only sugar and flour. Mix well and place mixture in lightly greased mug. In a separate bowl, combine contents of remaining bag. Using a pastry blender, cut in butter until mixture resembles fine crumbs. Place crumb mixture over apple mixture in mug. Bake in oven for 20 minutes. Enjoy!

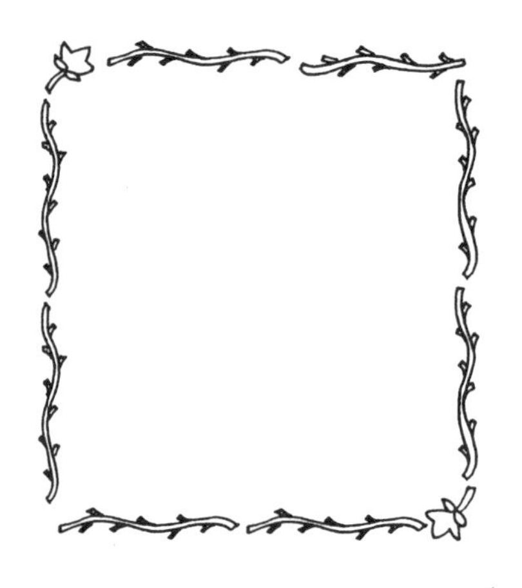

← fold →

You've
Been
Mugged!

MUG'EMS
by
CQ Products
www.cqproducts.com

You've
Been
Mugged!

MUG'EMS
by
CQ Products
www.cqproducts.com

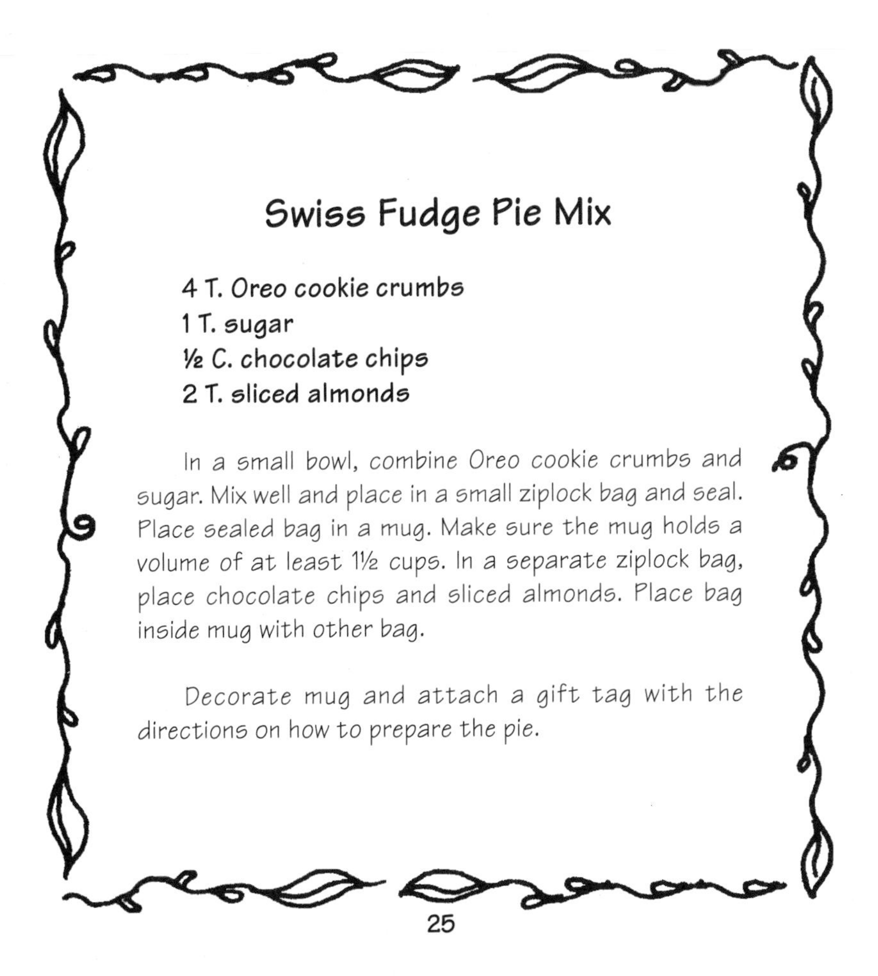

Swiss Fudge Pie Mix

4 T. Oreo cookie crumbs
1 T. sugar
½ C. chocolate chips
2 T. sliced almonds

In a small bowl, combine Oreo cookie crumbs and sugar. Mix well and place in a small ziplock bag and seal. Place sealed bag in a mug. Make sure the mug holds a volume of at least 1½ cups. In a separate ziplock bag, place chocolate chips and sliced almonds. Place bag inside mug with other bag.

Decorate mug and attach a gift tag with the directions on how to prepare the pie.

Gift tag directions: Swiss Fudge Pie

1 T. butter, melted
Swiss Fudge Pie Mix
½ C. sweetened condensed milk
1 egg yolk
½ tsp. vanilla

Preheat oven to 350°. In a small bowl, combine melted butter and contents of bag containing Oreo cookie crumbs. Mix well and press mixture into bottom and up side of lightly greased mug. Bake in oven for 6 to 8 minutes. Meanwhile, in a separate bowl, combine contents of remaining bag and sweetened condensed milk. Microwave mixture until chocolate chips are melted. Stir until blended and mix in egg yolk and vanilla. Pour chocolate mixture over crust in mug. Bake at 325° for 24 to 26 minutes. Let cool slightly. Enjoy!

Swiss Fudge Pie

1 T. butter, melted
Swiss Fudge Pie Mix
½ C. sweetened condensed milk
1 egg yolk
½ tsp. vanilla

Preheat oven to 350°. In a small bowl, combine melted butter and contents of bag containing Oreo cookie crumbs. Mix well and press mixture into bottom and up side of lightly greased mug. Bake in oven for 6 to 8 minutes. Meanwhile, in a separate bowl, combine contents of remaining bag and sweetened condensed milk. Microwave mixture until chocolate chips are melted. Stir until blended and mix in egg yolk and vanilla. Pour chocolate mixture over crust in mug. Bake at 325° for 24 to 26 minutes. Let cool slightly. Enjoy!

Swiss Fudge Pie

1 T. butter, melted
Swiss Fudge Pie Mix
½ C. sweetened condensed milk
1 egg yolk
½ tsp. vanilla

Preheat oven to 350°. In a small bowl, combine melted butter and contents of bag containing Oreo cookie crumbs. Mix well and press mixture into bottom and up side of lightly greased mug. Bake in oven for 6 to 8 minutes. Meanwhile, in a separate bowl, combine contents of remaining bag and sweetened condensed milk. Microwave mixture until chocolate chips are melted. Stir until blended and mix in egg yolk and vanilla. Pour chocolate mixture over crust in mug. Bake at 325° for 24 to 26 minutes. Let cool slightly. Enjoy!

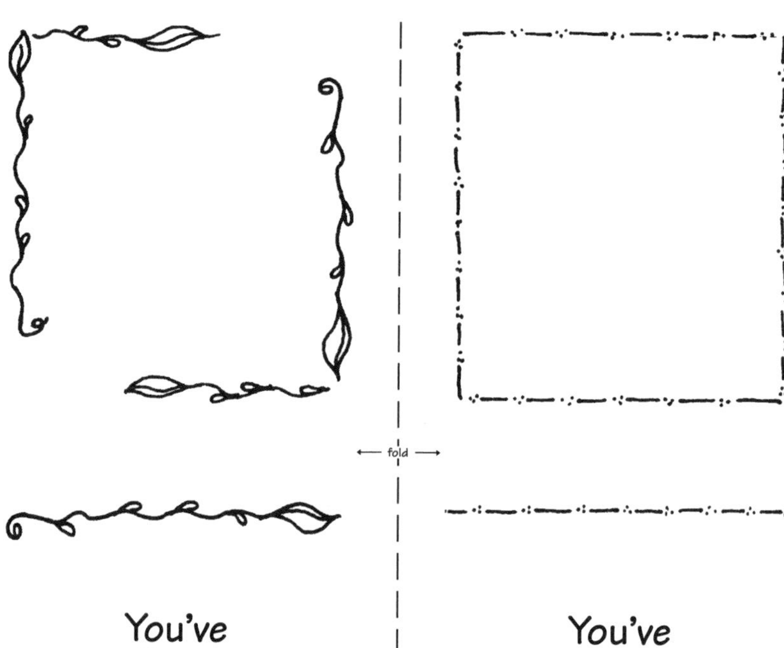

You've
Been
Mugged!

MUG'EMS
by
CQ Products
www.cqproducts.com

You've
Been
Mugged!

MUG'EMS
by
CQ Products
www.cqproducts.com

Swiss Fudge Pie

1 T. butter, melted
Swiss Fudge Pie Mix
½ C. sweetened condensed milk
1 egg yolk
½ tsp. vanilla

Preheat oven to 350°. In a small bowl, combine melted butter and contents of bag containing Oreo cookie crumbs. Mix well and press mixture into bottom and up side of lightly greased mug. Bake in oven for 6 to 8 minutes. Meanwhile, in a separate bowl, combine contents of remaining bag and sweetened condensed milk. Microwave mixture until chocolate chips are melted. Stir until blended and mix in egg yolk and vanilla. Pour chocolate mixture over crust in mug. Bake at 325° for 24 to 26 minutes. Let cool slightly. Enjoy!

Swiss Fudge Pie

1 T. butter, melted
Swiss Fudge Pie Mix
½ C. sweetened condensed milk
1 egg yolk
½ tsp. vanilla

Preheat oven to 350°. In a small bowl, combine melted butter and contents of bag containing Oreo cookie crumbs. Mix well and press mixture into bottom and up side of lightly greased mug. Bake in oven for 6 to 8 minutes. Meanwhile, in a separate bowl, combine contents of remaining bag and sweetened condensed milk. Microwave mixture until chocolate chips are melted. Stir until blended and mix in egg yolk and vanilla. Pour chocolate mixture over crust in mug. Bake at 325° for 24 to 26 minutes. Let cool slightly. Enjoy!

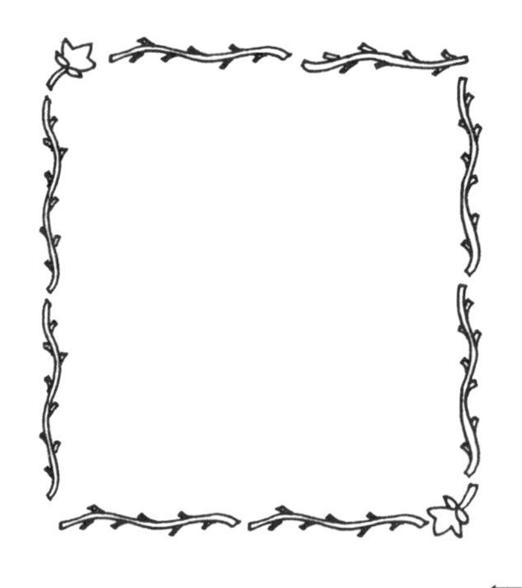

← fold →

You've Been Mugged!

MUG'EMS by CQ Products
www.cqproducts.com

You've Been Mugged!

MUG'EMS by CQ Products
www.cqproducts.com

Honey Cake Mix

1 T. brown sugar
¼ C. flour
¼ tsp. cinnamon
¼ tsp. allspice
¼ tsp. baking soda
½ tsp. baking powder
Pinch of ground cloves
1 T. finely chopped walnuts

In a small bowl, combine above ingredients. Mix well and place in a sandwich-size ziplock bag and seal. Place sealed bag in a mug. Make sure the mug holds a volume of at least 1½ cups.

Decorate mug and attach a gift tag with the directions on how to prepare the cake.

Gift tag directions:
Honey Cake

½ T. water
1 small egg
4 T. honey, divided
2 T. vegetable oil
Honey Cake Mix
1 T. butter, melted

Preheat oven to 350°. In a small bowl, combine water, egg, 2 tablespoons honey and vegetable oil. Mix well and add Honey Cake Mix from bag. Stir until smooth, about 1 minute. Pour batter into lightly greased mug and bake in oven for 15 to 18 minutes. Meanwhile, in a small bowl, combine remaining 2 tablespoons honey and melted butter. While cake is still warm, poke holes in top of cake and pour honey mixture over cake. Enjoy!

Honey Cake

½ T. water
1 small egg
4 T. honey, divided
2 T. vegetable oil
Honey Cake Mix
1 T. butter, melted

Preheat oven to 350°. In a small bowl, combine water, egg, 2 tablespoons honey and vegetable oil. Mix well and add Honey Cake Mix from bag. Stir until smooth, about 1 minute. Pour batter into lightly greased mug and bake in oven for 15 to 18 minutes. Meanwhile, in a small bowl, combine remaining 2 tablespoons honey and melted butter. While cake is still warm, poke holes in top of cake and pour honey mixture over cake. Enjoy!

Honey Cake

½ T. water
1 small egg
4 T. honey, divided
2 T. vegetable oil
Honey Cake Mix
1 T. butter, melted

Preheat oven to 350°. In a small bowl, combine water, egg, 2 tablespoons honey and vegetable oil. Mix well and add Honey Cake Mix from bag. Stir until smooth, about 1 minute. Pour batter into lightly greased mug and bake in oven for 15 to 18 minutes. Meanwhile, in a small bowl, combine remaining 2 tablespoons honey and melted butter. While cake is still warm, poke holes in top of cake and pour honey mixture over cake. Enjoy!

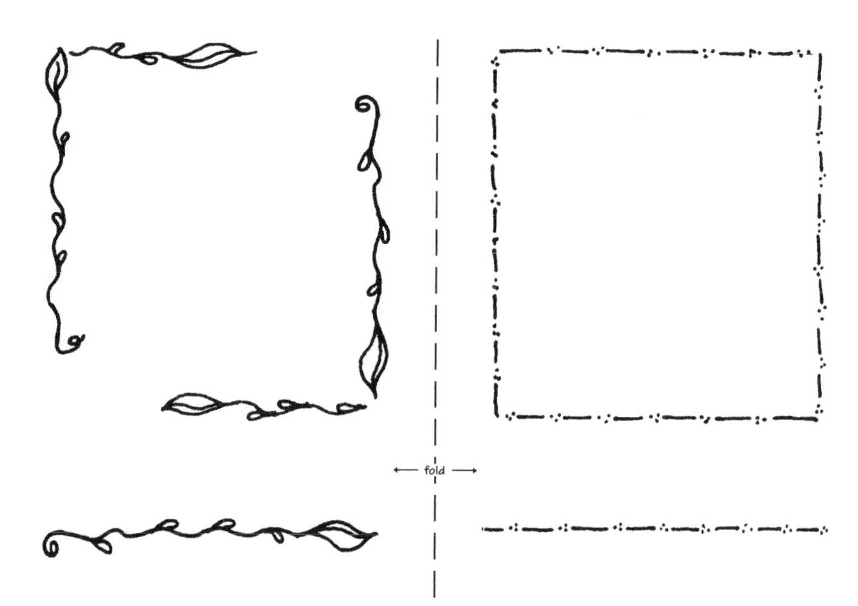

You've
Been
Mugged!

MUG'EMS
by
CQ Products
www.cqproducts.com

You've
Been
Mugged!

MUG'EMS
by
CQ Products
www.cqproducts.com

Honey Cake

½ T. water
1 small egg
4 T. honey, divided
2 T. vegetable oil
Honey Cake Mix
1 T. butter, melted

Preheat oven to 350°. In a small bowl, combine water, egg, 2 tablespoons honey and vegetable oil. Mix well and add Honey Cake Mix from bag. Stir until smooth, about 1 minute. Pour batter into lightly greased mug and bake in oven for 15 to 18 minutes. Meanwhile, in a small bowl, combine remaining 2 tablespoons honey and melted butter. While cake is still warm, poke holes in top of cake and pour honey mixture over cake. Enjoy!

Honey Cake

½ T. water
1 small egg
4 T. honey, divided
2 T. vegetable oil
Honey Cake Mix
1 T. butter, melted

Preheat oven to 350°. In a small bowl, combine water, egg, 2 tablespoons honey and vegetable oil. Mix well and add Honey Cake Mix from bag. Stir until smooth, about 1 minute. Pour batter into lightly greased mug and bake in oven for 15 to 18 minutes. Meanwhile, in a small bowl, combine remaining 2 tablespoons honey and melted butter. While cake is still warm, poke holes in top of cake and pour honey mixture over cake. Enjoy!

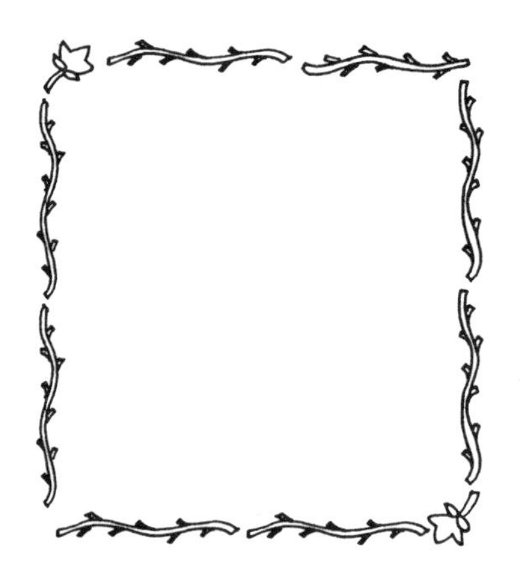

← fold →

You've
Been
Mugged!

You've
Been
Mugged!

MUG'EMS
by
CQ Products
www.cqproducts.com

German Apple Cake Mix

¼ C. flour
3 T. dark brown sugar
½ tsp. baking powder
¼ tsp. baking soda
½ tsp. cinnamon
Pinch of nutmeg
Pinch of ground cloves
1 T. finely chopped pecans

In a small bowl, combine above ingredients. Mix well and place in a sandwich-size ziplock bag and seal. Place sealed bag in a mug. Make sure the mug holds a volume of at least 1½ cups.

Decorate mug and attach a gift tag with the directions on how to prepare the cake.

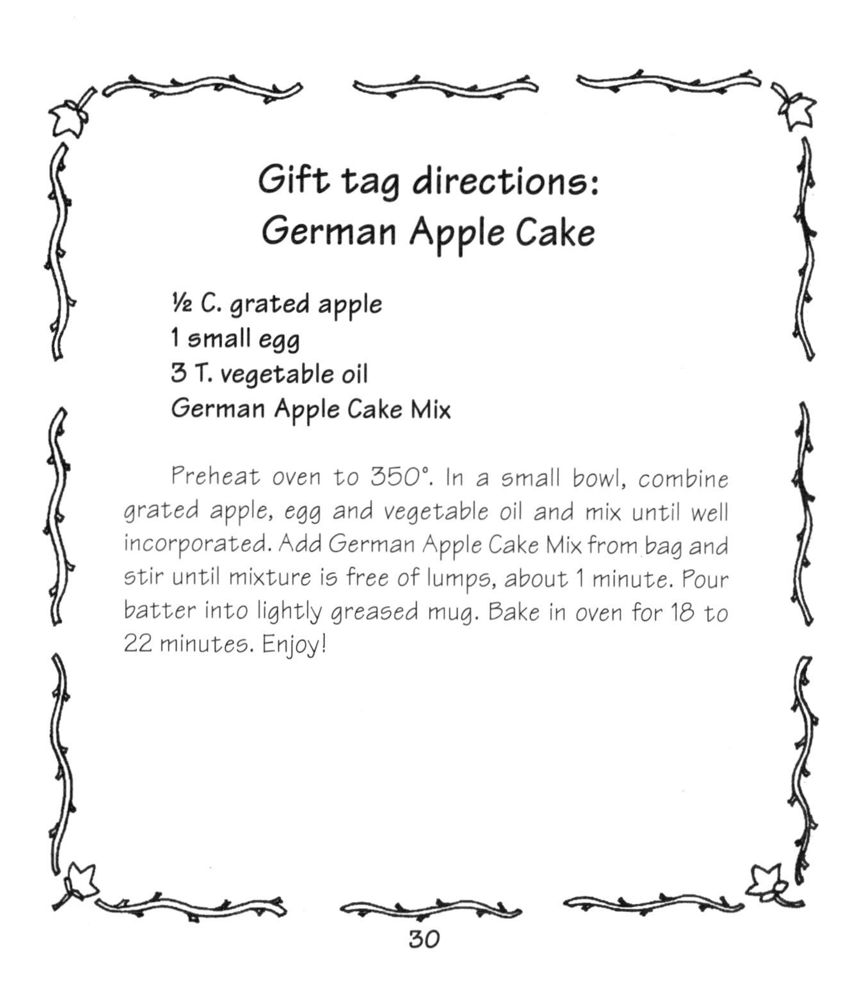

Gift tag directions: German Apple Cake

½ C. grated apple
1 small egg
3 T. vegetable oil
German Apple Cake Mix

Preheat oven to 350°. In a small bowl, combine grated apple, egg and vegetable oil and mix until well incorporated. Add German Apple Cake Mix from bag and stir until mixture is free of lumps, about 1 minute. Pour batter into lightly greased mug. Bake in oven for 18 to 22 minutes. Enjoy!

German Apple Cake

½ C. grated apple
1 small egg
3 T. vegetable oil
German Apple Cake Mix

Preheat oven to 350°. In a small bowl, combine grated apple, egg and vegetable oil and mix until well incorporated. Add German Apple Cake Mix from bag and stir until mixture is free of lumps, about 1 minute. Pour batter into lightly greased mug. Bake in oven for 18 to 22 minutes. Enjoy!

German Apple Cake

½ C. grated apple
1 small egg
3 T. vegetable oil
German Apple Cake Mix

Preheat oven to 350°. In a small bowl, combine grated apple, egg and vegetable oil and mix until well incorporated. Add German Apple Cake Mix from bag and stir until mixture is free of lumps, about 1 minute. Pour batter into lightly greased mug. Bake in oven for 18 to 22 minutes. Enjoy!

fold

You've
Been
Mugged!

MUG'EMS
by
CQ Products
www.cqproducts.com

You've
Been
Mugged!

MUG'EMS
by
CQ Products
www.cqproducts.com

German Apple Cake

½ C. grated apple
1 small egg
3 T. vegetable oil
German Apple Cake Mix

Preheat oven to 350°. In a small bowl, combine grated apple, egg and vegetable oil and mix until well incorporated. Add German Apple Cake Mix from bag and stir until mixture is free of lumps, about 1 minute. Pour batter into lightly greased mug. Bake in oven for 18 to 22 minutes. Enjoy!

German Apple Cake

½ C. grated apple
1 small egg
3 T. vegetable oil
German Apple Cake Mix

Preheat oven to 350°. In a small bowl, combine grated apple, egg and vegetable oil and mix until well incorporated. Add German Apple Cake Mix from bag and stir until mixture is free of lumps, about 1 minute. Pour batter into lightly greased mug. Bake in oven for 18 to 22 minutes. Enjoy!

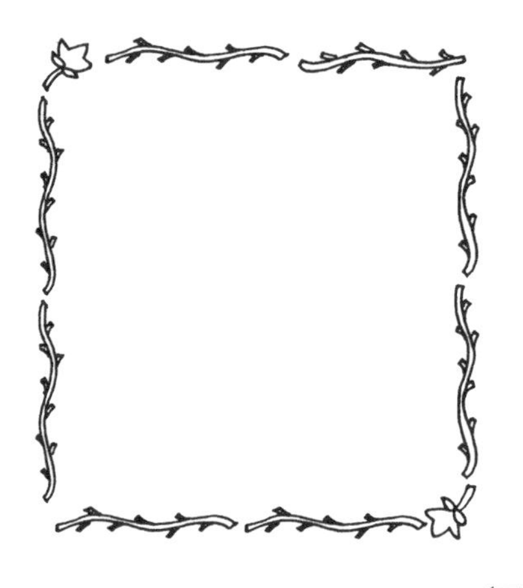

← fold →

You've
Been
Mugged!

MUG'EMS
by
CQ Products
www.cqproducts.com

You've
Been
Mugged!

MUG'EMS
by
CQ Products
www.cqproducts.com

Hot Spiced Cider Mix

1 T. dark brown sugar
1 cinnamon stick
2 or 3 whole cloves
Pinch of allspice

In a small bowl, combine above ingredients. Mix well and place in a sandwich-size ziplock bag and seal. Place sealed bag in a mug. Make sure the mug holds a volume of at least 1½ cups.

Decorate mug and attach a gift tag with the directions on how to prepare the cider.

Gift tag directions:
Hot Spiced Cider

1 C. apple cider
1 tsp. honey
Hot Spiced Cider Mix
Orange wedge for garnish, optional

Place apple cider and honey in mug. Heat in microwave until almost boiling. Remove from microwave and add Hot Spiced Cider Mix from bag. Mix well and let steep for about 5 minutes. If desired, garnish with an orange wedge. Enjoy!

Hot Spiced Cider

1 C. apple cider
1 tsp. honey
Hot Spiced Cider Mix
Orange wedge for garnish, optional

Place apple cider and honey in mug. Heat in microwave until almost boiling. Remove from microwave and add Hot Spiced Cider Mix from bag. Mix well and let steep for about 5 minutes. If desired, garnish with an orange wedge. Enjoy!

Hot Spiced Cider

1 C. apple cider
1 tsp. honey
Hot Spiced Cider Mix
Orange wedge for garnish, optional

Place apple cider and honey in mug. Heat in microwave until almost boiling. Remove from microwave and add Hot Spiced Cider Mix from bag. Mix well and let steep for about 5 minutes. If desired, garnish with an orange wedge. Enjoy!

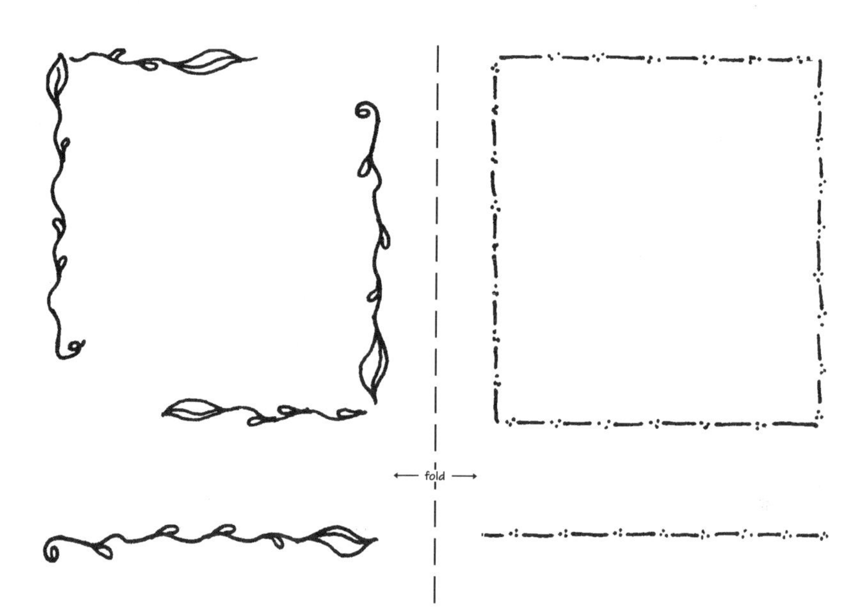

You've
Been
Mugged!

MUG'EMS
by
CQ Products
www.cqproducts.com

You've
Been
Mugged!

MUG'EMS
by
CQ Products
www.cqproducts.com

Hot Spiced Cider

1 C. apple cider
1 tsp. honey
Hot Spiced Cider Mix
Orange wedge for garnish, optional

Place apple cider and honey in mug. Heat in microwave until almost boiling. Remove from microwave and add Hot Spiced Cider Mix from bag. Mix well and let steep for about 5 minutes. If desired, garnish with an orange wedge. Enjoy!

Hot Spiced Cider

1 C. apple cider
1 tsp. honey
Hot Spiced Cider Mix
Orange wedge for garnish, optional

Place apple cider and honey in mug. Heat in microwave until almost boiling. Remove from microwave and add Hot Spiced Cider Mix from bag. Mix well and let steep for about 5 minutes. If desired, garnish with an orange wedge. Enjoy!

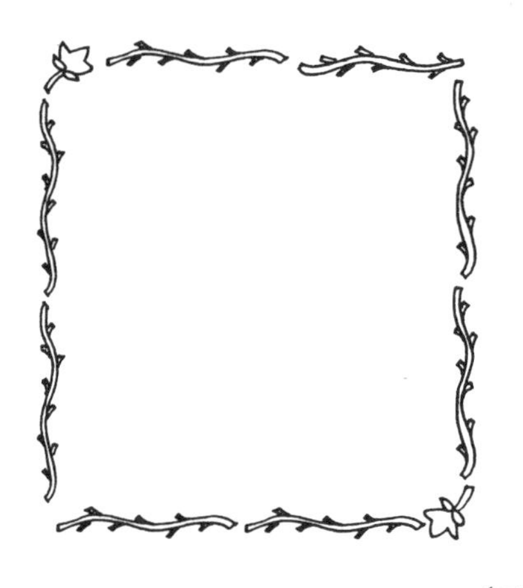

← fold →

You've
Been
Mugged!

You've
Been
Mugged!

MUG'EMS
by
CQ Products
www.cqproducts.com

Grasshopper Pie Mix

4 T. Oreo cookie crumbs
½ T. sugar
1 C. miniature marshmallows

In a small bowl, combine Oreo cookie crumbs and sugar. Mix well and place in a small ziplock bag and seal. Place sealed bag in a mug. Make sure the mug holds a volume of at least 1½ cups. In a separate ziplock bag, place miniature marshmallows. Place bag inside mug with other bag.

Decorate mug and attach a gift tag with the directions on how to prepare the pie.

Gift tag directions:
Grasshopper Pie

1 T. butter, melted
Grasshopper Pie Mix
2 T. whole milk
1 T. Crème de Menthe liqueur
¼ C. whipped cream

Preheat oven to 350°. To make crust, in a small bowl, combine melted butter and contents of bag containing Oreo cookie crumbs. Mix well and press mixture into the bottom and halfway up sides of lightly greased mug. Bake in oven for 6 to 8 minutes. Meanwhile, in a glass measuring cup, combine milk and marshmallows from remaining bag. Microwave until marshmallows are melted and stir until smooth. Add Crème de Menthe and mix well. Fold in whipped cream. Allow crust to cool slightly and pour marshmallow mixture over crust in mug. Chill in refrigerator at least 3 hours. Enjoy!

Grasshopper Pie

1 T. butter, melted
Grasshopper Pie Mix
2 T. whole milk
1 T. Crème de Menthe liqueur
¼ C. whipped cream

Preheat oven to 350°. To make crust, in a small bowl, combine melted butter and contents of bag containing Oreo cookie crumbs. Mix well and press mixture into the bottom and halfway up sides of lightly greased mug. Bake in oven for 6 to 8 minutes. Meanwhile, in a glass measuring cup, combine milk and marshmallows from remaining bag. Microwave until marshmallows are melted and stir until smooth. Add Crème de Menthe and mix well. Fold in whipped cream. Allow crust to cool slightly and pour marshmallow mixture over crust in mug. Chill in refrigerator at least 3 hours. Enjoy!

Grasshopper Pie

1 T. butter, melted
Grasshopper Pie Mix
2 T. whole milk
1 T. Crème de Menthe liqueur
¼ C. whipped cream

Preheat oven to 350°. To make crust, in a small bowl, combine melted butter and contents of bag containing Oreo cookie crumbs. Mix well and press mixture into the bottom and halfway up sides of lightly greased mug. Bake in oven for 6 to 8 minutes. Meanwhile, in a glass measuring cup, combine milk and marshmallows from remaining bag. Microwave until marshmallows are melted and stir until smooth. Add Crème de Menthe and mix well. Fold in whipped cream. Allow crust to cool slightly and pour marshmallow mixture over crust in mug. Chill in refrigerator at least 3 hours. Enjoy!

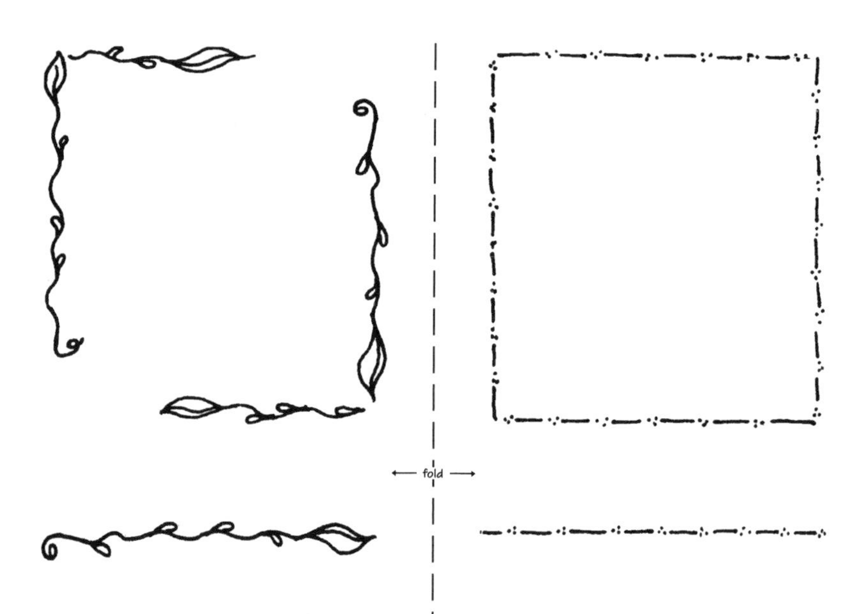

You've
Been
Mugged!

MUG'EMS
by
CQ Products
www.cqproducts.com

You've
Been
Mugged!

MUG'EMS
by
CQ Products
www.cqproducts.com

Grasshopper Pie

1 T. butter, melted
Grasshopper Pie Mix
2 T. whole milk
1 T. Crème de Menthe liqueur
¼ C. whipped cream

Preheat oven to 350°. To make crust, in a small bowl, combine melted butter and contents of bag containing Oreo cookie crumbs. Mix well and press mixture into the bottom and halfway up sides of lightly greased mug. Bake in oven for 6 to 8 minutes. Meanwhile, in a glass measuring cup, combine milk and marshmallows from remaining bag. Microwave until marshmallows are melted and stir until smooth. Add Crème de Menthe and mix well. Fold in whipped cream. Allow crust to cool slightly and pour marshmallow mixture over crust in mug. Chill in refrigerator at least 3 hours. Enjoy!

Grasshopper Pie

1 T. butter, melted
Grasshopper Pie Mix
2 T. whole milk
1 T. Crème de Menthe liqueur
¼ C. whipped cream

Preheat oven to 350°. To make crust, in a small bowl, combine melted butter and contents of bag containing Oreo cookie crumbs. Mix well and press mixture into the bottom and halfway up sides of lightly greased mug. Bake in oven for 6 to 8 minutes. Meanwhile, in a glass measuring cup, combine milk and marshmallows from remaining bag. Microwave until marshmallows are melted and stir until smooth. Add Crème de Menthe and mix well. Fold in whipped cream. Allow crust to cool slightly and pour marshmallow mixture over crust in mug. Chill in refrigerator at least 3 hours. Enjoy!

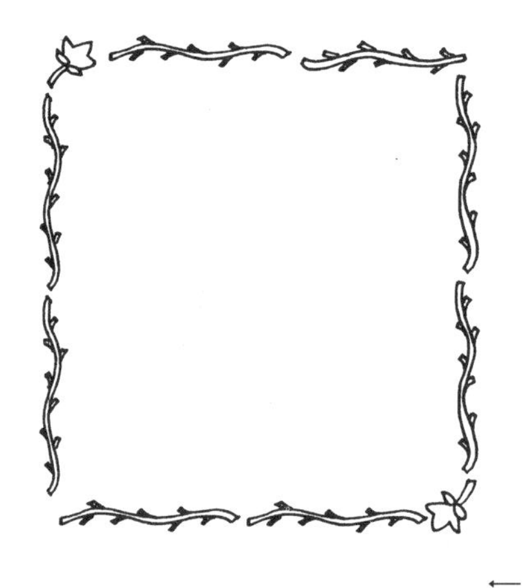

← fold →

You've
Been
Mugged!

MUG'EMS
by
CQ Products
www.cqproducts.com

You've
Been
Mugged!

MUG'EMS
by
CQ Products
www.cqproducts.com

Plum Pudding Mix

1 C. dried, cubed bread
2 T. flour
1 T. brown sugar
½ tsp. baking soda
¼ tsp. cinnamon
Pinch of salt
Pinch of nutmeg
1 T. raisins
1 T. currants

In a small bowl, combine above ingredients. Mix well and place in a sandwich-size ziplock bag and seal. Place sealed bag in a mug. Make sure the mug holds a volume of at least 1½ cups.

Decorate mug and attach a gift tag with the directions on how to prepare the pudding.

Gift tag directions:
Plum Pudding

Plum Pudding Mix
⅓ C. orange juice
1 T. butter
1 T. molasses
1 egg yolk
Additional butter
Sugar
Brown sugar

Preheat oven to 325°. Place Plum Pudding Mix from bag in a small bowl. Pour orange juice over ingredients and let bread crumbs absorb orange juice for 3 to 5 minutes. In a glass measuring cup, place butter and molasses. Heat in microwave until butter and molasses are melted. Pour melted mixture over bread crumb mixture and add egg yolk. Mix until blended. Lightly coat mug with butter and sprinkle with sugar to coat the bottom and sides. Pour mixture into mug. Place mug in a pot. Fill pot with water until water level is halfway up side of mug. Cover mug with a saucer and place pot with mug in oven and bake for 25 to 30 minutes. Let cool slightly and top with a little butter and a sprinkle of brown sugar. Enjoy!

Plum Pudding

Plum Pudding Mix
1/3 C. orange juice
1 T. butter
1 T. molasses
1 egg yolk
Additional butter
Sugar
Brown sugar

Preheat oven to 325°. Place Plum Pudding Mix from bag in a small bowl. Pour orange juice over ingredients and let bread crumbs absorb orange juice for 3 to 5 minutes. In a glass measuring cup, place butter and molasses. Heat in microwave until butter and molasses are melted. Pour melted mixture over bread crumb mixture and add egg yolk. Mix until blended. Lightly coat mug with butter and sprinkle with sugar to coat the bottom and sides. Pour mixture into mug. Place mug in a pot. Fill pot with water until water level is halfway up side of mug. Cover mug with a saucer and place pot with mug in oven and bake for 25 to 30 minutes. Let cool slightly and top with a little butter and a sprinkle of brown sugar. Enjoy!

Plum Pudding

Plum Pudding Mix
1/3 C. orange juice
1 T. butter
1 T. molasses
1 egg yolk
Additional butter
Sugar
Brown sugar

Preheat oven to 325°. Place Plum Pudding Mix from bag in a small bowl. Pour orange juice over ingredients and let bread crumbs absorb orange juice for 3 to 5 minutes. In a glass measuring cup, place butter and molasses. Heat in microwave until butter and molasses are melted. Pour melted mixture over bread crumb mixture and add egg yolk. Mix until blended. Lightly coat mug with butter and sprinkle with sugar to coat the bottom and sides. Pour mixture into mug. Place mug in a pot. Fill pot with water until water level is halfway up side of mug. Cover mug with a saucer and place pot with mug in oven and bake for 25 to 30 minutes. Let cool slightly and top with a little butter and a sprinkle of brown sugar. Enjoy!

fold

You've
Been
Mugged!

MUG'EMS
by
CQ Products
www.cqproducts.com

You've
Been
Mugged!

MUG'EMS
by
CQ Products
www.cqproducts.com

Plum Pudding

Plum Pudding Mix
⅓ C. orange juice
1 T. butter
1 T. molasses
1 egg yolk
Additional butter
Sugar
Brown sugar

Preheat oven to 325°. Place Plum Pudding Mix from bag in a small bowl. Pour orange juice over ingredients and let bread crumbs absorb orange juice for 3 to 5 minutes. In a glass measuring cup, place butter and molasses. Heat in microwave until butter and molasses are melted. Pour melted mixture over bread crumb mixture and add egg yolk. Mix until blended. Lightly coat mug with butter and sprinkle with sugar to coat the bottom and sides. Pour mixture into mug. Place mug in a pot. Fill pot with water until water level is halfway up side of mug. Cover mug with a saucer and place pot with mug in oven and bake for 25 to 30 minutes. Let cool slightly and top with a little butter and a sprinkle of brown sugar. Enjoy!

Plum Pudding

Plum Pudding Mix
⅓ C. orange juice
1 T. butter
1 T. molasses
1 egg yolk
Additional butter
Sugar
Brown sugar

Preheat oven to 325°. Place Plum Pudding Mix from bag in a small bowl. Pour orange juice over ingredients and let bread crumbs absorb orange juice for 3 to 5 minutes. In a glass measuring cup, place butter and molasses. Heat in microwave until butter and molasses are melted. Pour melted mixture over bread crumb mixture and add egg yolk. Mix until blended. Lightly coat mug with butter and sprinkle with sugar to coat the bottom and sides. Pour mixture into mug. Place mug in a pot. Fill pot with water until water level is halfway up side of mug. Cover mug with a saucer and place pot with mug in oven and bake for 25 to 30 minutes. Let cool slightly and top with a little butter and a sprinkle of brown sugar. Enjoy!

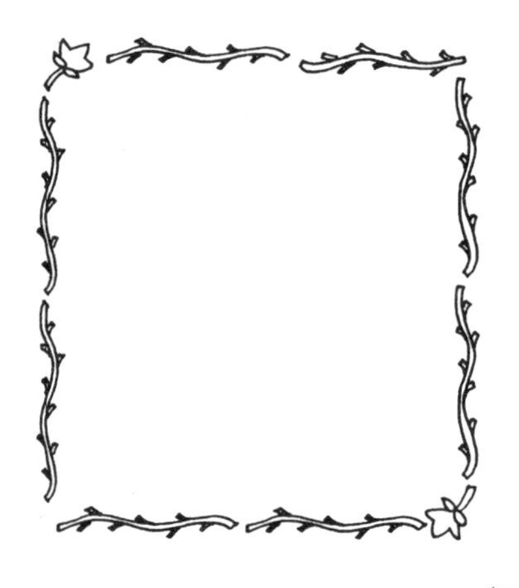

← fold →

You've
Been
Mugged!

MUG'EMS
by
CQ Products
www.cqproducts.com

You've
Been
Mugged!

MUG'EMS
by
CQ Products
www.cqproducts.com

Nutty Currant Stuffing Mix

1 C. dried, cubed bread
1 T. chopped walnuts
1½ tsp. chicken bouillon
2 tsp. dried parsley flakes
1 tsp. celery flakes
¼ tsp. dried onion flakes
1½ T. currants
Pinch of salt
⅛ tsp. pepper

In a small bowl, combine above ingredients. Mix well and place in a sandwich-size ziplock bag and seal. Place sealed bag in a mug. Make sure the mug holds a volume of at least 1½ cups.

Decorate mug and attach a gift tag with the directions on how to prepare the stuffing.

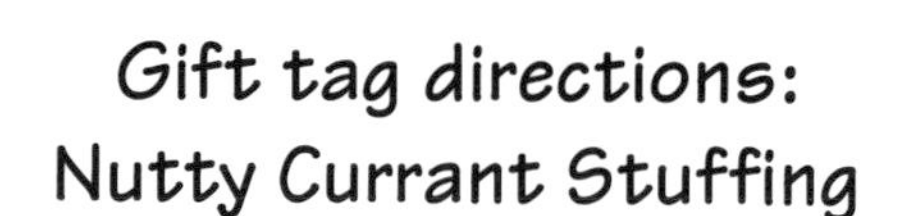

Gift tag directions: Nutty Currant Stuffing

Nutty Currant Stuffing Mix
1 T. butter
⅓ C. water

Preheat oven to 350°. In a small bowl, place Nutty Currant Stuffing Mix from bag. In a glass measuring cup, place butter and water. Heat in microwave until butter is melted. Pour melted butter mixture over ingredients in bowl. Toss until bread crumbs are moistened. Transfer mixture to lightly greased mug. Loosely cover mug with a small piece of aluminum foil. Bake in oven for 15 minutes. Let cool slightly. Enjoy!

Nutty Currant Stuffing

Nutty Currant Stuffing Mix
1 T. butter
⅓ C. water

Preheat oven to 350°. In a small bowl, place Nutty Currant Stuffing Mix from bag. In a glass measuring cup, place butter and water. Heat in microwave until butter is melted. Pour melted butter mixture over ingredients in bowl. Toss until bread crumbs are moistened. Transfer mixture to lightly greased mug. Loosely cover mug with a small piece of aluminum foil. Bake in oven for 15 minutes. Let cool slightly. Enjoy!

Nutty Currant Stuffing

Nutty Currant Stuffing Mix
1 T. butter
⅓ C. water

Preheat oven to 350°. In a small bowl, place Nutty Currant Stuffing Mix from bag. In a glass measuring cup, place butter and water. Heat in microwave until butter is melted. Pour melted butter mixture over ingredients in bowl. Toss until bread crumbs are moistened. Transfer mixture to lightly greased mug. Loosely cover mug with a small piece of aluminum foil. Bake in oven for 15 minutes. Let cool slightly. Enjoy!

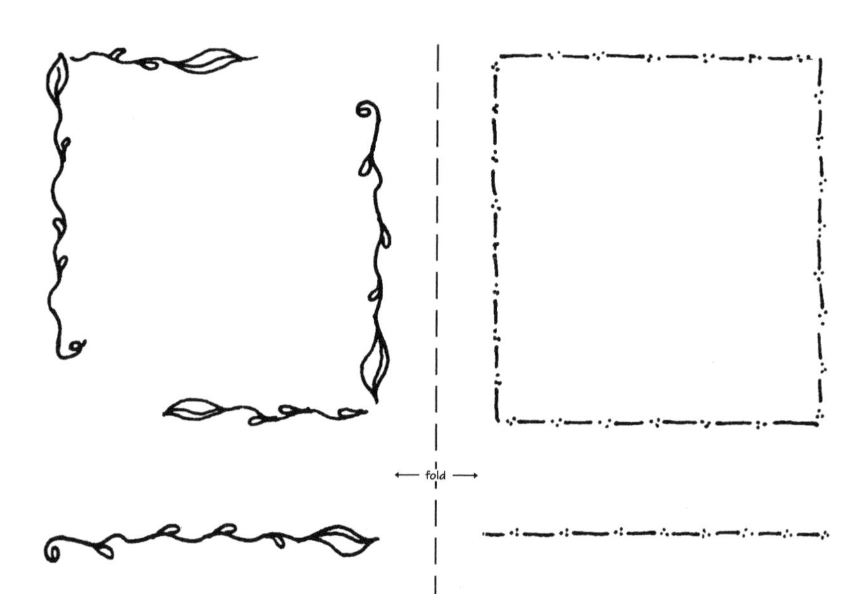

You've
Been
Mugged!

MUG'EMS
by
CQ Products
www.cqproducts.com

You've
Been
Mugged!

MUG'EMS
by
CQ Products
www.cqproducts.com

Nutty Currant Stuffing

Nutty Currant Stuffing Mix
1 T. butter
⅓ C. water

Preheat oven to 350°. In a small bowl, place Nutty Currant Stuffing Mix from bag. In a glass measuring cup, place butter and water. Heat in microwave until butter is melted. Pour melted butter mixture over ingredients in bowl. Toss until bread crumbs are moistened. Transfer mixture to lightly greased mug. Loosely cover mug with a small piece of aluminum foil. Bake in oven for 15 minutes. Let cool slightly. Enjoy!

Nutty Currant Stuffing

Nutty Currant Stuffing Mix
1 T. butter
⅓ C. water

Preheat oven to 350°. In a small bowl, place Nutty Currant Stuffing Mix from bag. In a glass measuring cup, place butter and water. Heat in microwave until butter is melted. Pour melted butter mixture over ingredients in bowl. Toss until bread crumbs are moistened. Transfer mixture to lightly greased mug. Loosely cover mug with a small piece of aluminum foil. Bake in oven for 15 minutes. Let cool slightly. Enjoy!

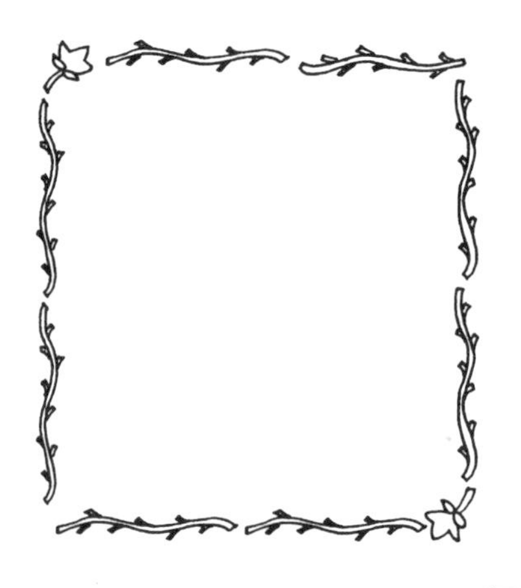

← fold →

You've
Been
Mugged!

MUG'EMS
by
CQ Products
www.cqproducts.com

You've
Been
Mugged!

MUG'EMS
by
CQ Products
www.cqproducts.com

Clam Chowder Mix

1½ T. dry potato flakes
2 T. dried hash browns
½ tsp. salt
¼ tsp. pepper
½ tsp. dried onion flakes
1 tsp. celery flakes
¾ tsp. dried dillweed
2 T. Knorr Classic white sauce mix

In a small bowl, combine above ingredients. Mix well and place in a sandwich-size ziplock bag and seal. Place sealed bag in a mug. Make sure the mug holds a volume of at least 1½ cups.

Decorate mug and attach a gift tag with the directions on how to prepare the chowder.

Gift tag directions:
Clam Chowder

Clam Chowder Mix
¾ C. milk
½ T. butter
2 T. clams
Crackers, optional

Place Clam Chowder Mix from bag in mug. In a small saucepan over medium heat, combine milk and butter. Bring to a low simmer and pour over ingredients in mug. Cover mug and let sit for 5 minutes. Add clams and mix well. Place mug in microwave for 1½ to 2 minutes, until heated throughout. If desired, crumble crackers over chowder. Enjoy!

Clam Chowder

Clam Chowder Mix
¾ C. milk
½ T. butter
2 T. clams
Crackers, optional

Place Clam Chowder Mix from bag in mug. In a small saucepan over medium heat, combine milk and butter. Bring to a low simmer and pour over ingredients in mug. Cover mug and let sit for 5 minutes. Add clams and mix well. Place mug in microwave for 1½ to 2 minutes, until heated throughout. If desired, crumble crackers over chowder. Enjoy!

Clam Chowder

Clam Chowder Mix
¾ C. milk
½ T. butter
2 T. clams
Crackers, optional

Place Clam Chowder Mix from bag in mug. In a small saucepan over medium heat, combine milk and butter. Bring to a low simmer and pour over ingredients in mug. Cover mug and let sit for 5 minutes. Add clams and mix well. Place mug in microwave for 1½ to 2 minutes, until heated throughout. If desired, crumble crackers over chowder. Enjoy!

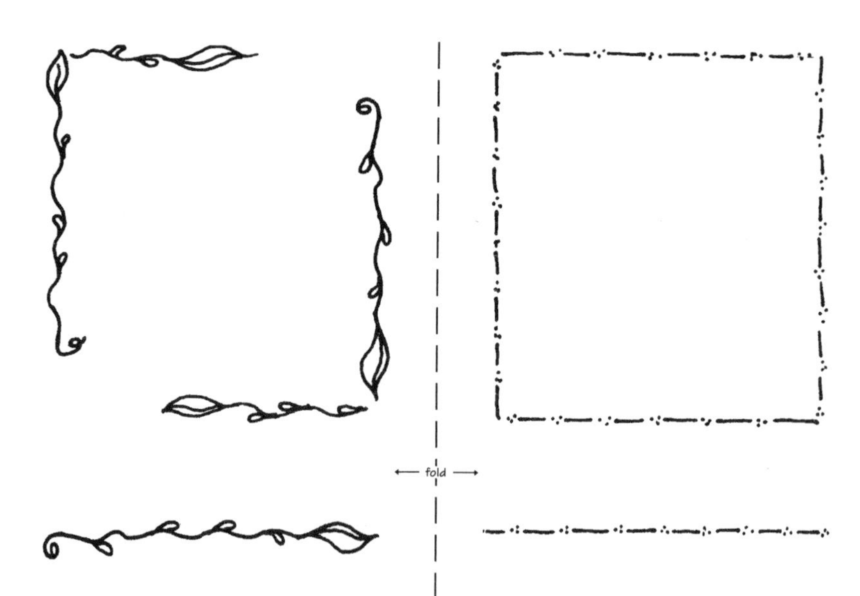

You've
Been
Mugged!

MUG'EMS
by
CQ Products
www.cqproducts.com

You've
Been
Mugged!

MUG'EMS
by
CQ Products
www.cqproducts.com

Clam Chowder

Clam Chowder Mix
¾ C. milk
½ T. butter
2 T. clams
Crackers, optional

Place Clam Chowder Mix from bag in mug. In a small saucepan over medium heat, combine milk and butter. Bring to a low simmer and pour over ingredients in mug. Cover mug and let sit for 5 minutes. Add clams and mix well. Place mug in microwave for 1½ to 2 minutes, until heated throughout. If desired, crumble crackers over chowder. Enjoy!

Clam Chowder

Clam Chowder Mix
¾ C. milk
½ T. butter
2 T. clams
Crackers, optional

Place Clam Chowder Mix from bag in mug. In a small saucepan over medium heat, combine milk and butter. Bring to a low simmer and pour over ingredients in mug. Cover mug and let sit for 5 minutes. Add clams and mix well. Place mug in microwave for 1½ to 2 minutes, until heated throughout. If desired, crumble crackers over chowder. Enjoy!

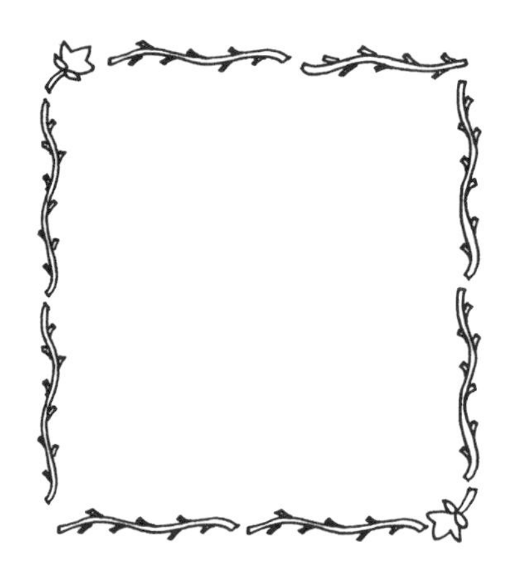

fold

You've
Been
Mugged!

MUG'EMS
by
CQ Products
www.cqproducts.com

You've
Been
Mugged!

MUG'EMS
by
CQ Products
www.cqproducts.com

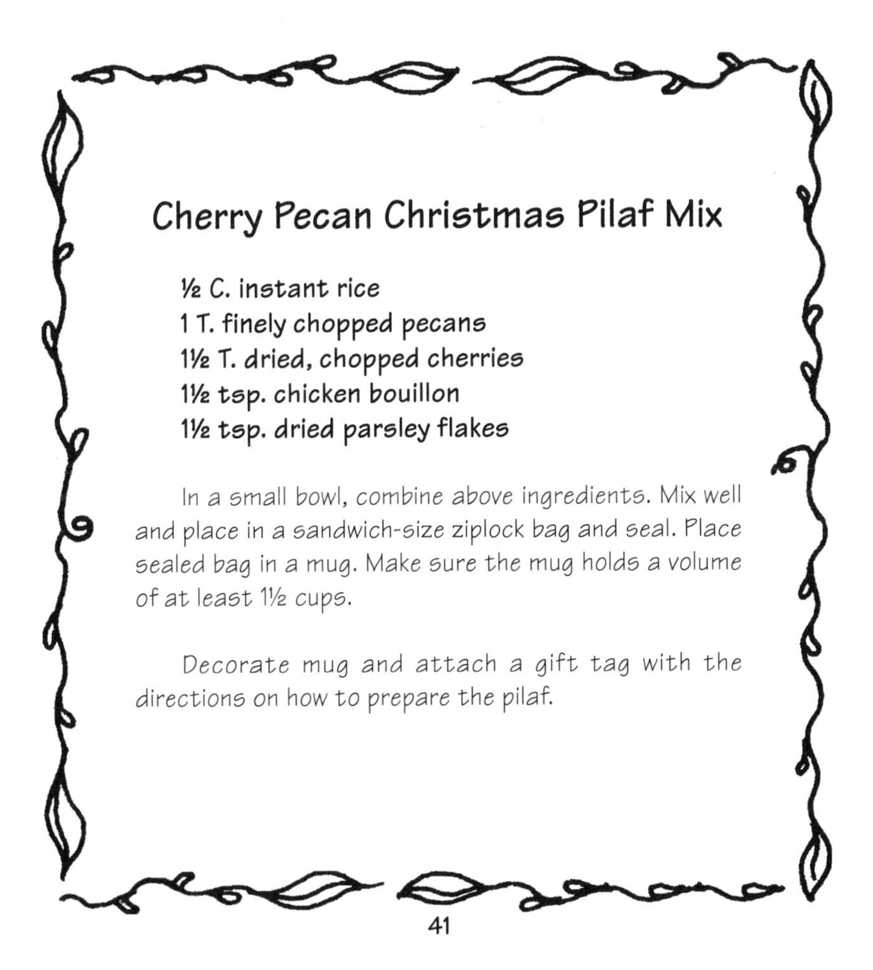

Cherry Pecan Christmas Pilaf Mix

½ C. instant rice
1 T. finely chopped pecans
1½ T. dried, chopped cherries
1½ tsp. chicken bouillon
1½ tsp. dried parsley flakes

In a small bowl, combine above ingredients. Mix well and place in a sandwich-size ziplock bag and seal. Place sealed bag in a mug. Make sure the mug holds a volume of at least 1½ cups.

Decorate mug and attach a gift tag with the directions on how to prepare the pilaf.

Gift tag directions:
Cherry Pecan Christmas Pilaf

⅔ C. water
1 T. butter
Cherry Pecan Christmas Pilaf Mix

Place water and butter in mug. Microwave on high until mixture is boiling. Remove from microwave and add Cherry Pecan Christmas Pilaf Mix from bag. Mix until well incorporated. Cover and let sit for 6 to 10 minutes. Fluff lightly with a fork. Enjoy!

Cherry Pecan Christmas Pilaf

⅔ C. water
1 T. butter
Cherry Pecan Christmas Pilaf Mix

Place water and butter in mug. Microwave on high until mixture is boiling. Remove from microwave and add Cherry Pecan Christmas Pilaf Mix from bag. Mix until well incorporated. Cover and let sit for 6 to 10 minutes. Fluff lightly with a fork. Enjoy!

Cherry Pecan Christmas Pilaf

⅔ C. water
1 T. butter
Cherry Pecan Christmas Pilaf Mix

Place water and butter in mug. Microwave on high until mixture is boiling. Remove from microwave and add Cherry Pecan Christmas Pilaf Mix from bag. Mix until well incorporated. Cover and let sit for 6 to 10 minutes. Fluff lightly with a fork. Enjoy!

MUG'EMS by CQ Products
www.cqproducts.com

MUG'EMS by CQ Products
www.cqproducts.com

Cherry Pecan Christmas Pilaf

⅔ C. water
1 T. butter
Cherry Pecan Christmas Pilaf Mix

Place water and butter in mug. Microwave on high until mixture is boiling. Remove from microwave and add Cherry Pecan Christmas Pilaf Mix from bag. Mix until well incorporated. Cover and let sit for 6 to 10 minutes. Fluff lightly with a fork. Enjoy!

Cherry Pecan Christmas Pilaf

⅔ C. water
1 T. butter
Cherry Pecan Christmas Pilaf Mix

Place water and butter in mug. Microwave on high until mixture is boiling. Remove from microwave and add Cherry Pecan Christmas Pilaf Mix from bag. Mix until well incorporated. Cover and let sit for 6 to 10 minutes. Fluff lightly with a fork. Enjoy!

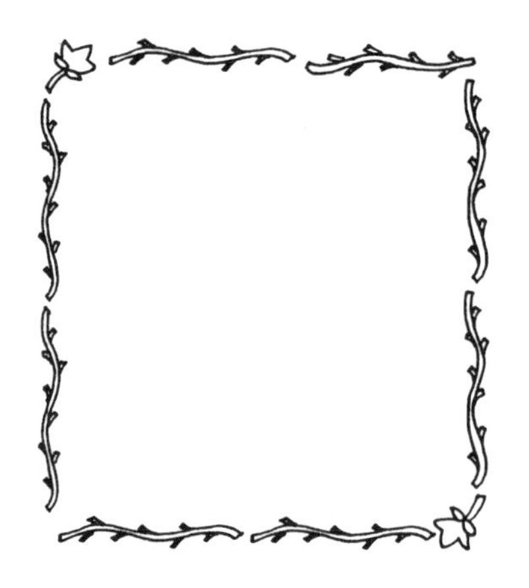

← fold →

You've
Been
Mugged!

MUG'EMS
by
CQ Products
www.cqproducts.com

You've
Been
Mugged!

MUG'EMS
by
CQ Products
www.cqproducts.com

Index

Tips on Preparing & Decorating:

- Holiday themed food-safe bags, normally found at your local craft store, add a nice touch to your gift.
- It is often easier to place the open bag in the mug first. Then pour the ingredients into the open bag and seal. If needed, use a thin paper plate as a funnel.
- Before decorating the bag with ribbon, raffia or a fabric strip, first close the bag with a rubber band or twist tie.
- Add your personalized greeting to one side of the gift tag then fold in half. Punch a hole into the corner of the tag and use ribbon, raffia, twine, lace or a fabric strip to attach the tag to the mug.
- Mug 'Ems make great gifts for Mother's Day, birthdays, holidays or a sick friend. Accessorize the gift by attaching a small gift such as a stirring spoon, fork or hot pad to the mug.

To purchase more
books by
CQ Products
see your local
gift or craft store!
Or call to order a
FREE catalog at
866-804-9892
CQ Products
507 Industrial St.
Waverly, IA 50677
www.cqproducts.com • fax 800-886-7496